ENCORE LEADERSHIP
— WORKBOOK —

*Transforming Time, Talent and Treasure
Into a Legacy that Matters*

Jylla Moore Tearte, PhD

CRYSTAL STAIRS PUBLISHERS

Copyright © 2013 by Jylla Moore Tearte, PhD

All rights reserved. No part of this book may be reproduced or transmitted in any form or by any means, electronic or mechanical, including photocopying, recording, or by any information storage and retrieval system, without the written permission from the author, except for the inclusion of brief quotations in a review. For information, contact:

Crystal Stairs, Inc., P. O. Box 12215, Atlanta, GA, USA 30355
EncoreLeadership@Crystal-Stairs.com • www.Crystal-Stairs.com

CRYSTAL STAIRS PUBLISHERS

This workbook is intended for use by individuals who are engaged in Encore Leadership coaching programs offered by Crystal Stairs, Inc. or its assigned agents. It is a companion workbook to *Encore Leadership: Transforming Time, Talent and Treasure into a Legacy that Matters*. (Trade Paperback ISBN: 978-0-9722441-4-5). Other use is strictly prohibited without the expressed written permission of Crystal Stairs, Inc. — www.Crystal-Stairs.com. The author and publisher shall have neither liability nor responsibility to anyone with respect to any loss or damage caused, or alleged to be caused, directly or indirectly, by the information contained in this book. Although the author and publisher have made every attempt to ensure accuracy and completeness of information presented, they assume no responsibility for errors, inaccuracies, omissions, or inconsistencies.

Original Cover Design by The Onyx Collection Media Group
Journal Cover Design by the Ink Studio

ENCORE LEADERSHIP WORKBOOK: Transforming Time, Talent and Treasure Into a Legacy that Matters
By Jylla Moore Tearte, PhD

ISBN (Trade Paperback)   978-1-9401310-3-0
ISBN (Fillable PDF eBook)   978-1-9401310-2-3

All Encore Leadership companion materials available at www.EncoreLeadership.com

Printed in the United States of America

Dedication

This workbook is dedicated to all of the brave hearts and souls who have reached a "Transition Tipping Point" and are ready to do legacy work that matters! Thank you for engaging as an Encore Leader on your amazing journey!

Jylla

Contents

Introduction ix

SECTION I: PERSONAL REFLECTION 1

Tools for Reflection 3
Situations 3
Quality of Life 100™ 9
From Sick and Tired to Strong and Tenacious 15
Goals Inventory 18

SECTION II: PREPARING FOR THE TRANSFORMATION JOURNEY 21

Exercises to Help You Shift on Your Journey 23
Sheroes and Heroes 24
Encore Leadership Attributes 28
    Attributes to Reframe Your Life 29
    Attributes to Renew Your Life 30
Halftime 31
The Good Life Inventory 35
The Story of Your Life 38
Visioning of Future Self 43

SECTION III: THE ENCORE LEADERSHIP PROCESS© 49

4 Stages, 12 Steps 51
The Transition Tipping Point 52
Poignant, Provocative and Pivotal Questions 57
Encore Leadership Mindset 62

The 12 Steps of Transformation.. 65

1. Document Your Journey.. 67
   - The Transition Journey Exercise... 70
   - The Big 5 Game Changers.. 74
   - Lifeline Exercise 76
   - Bucket List 77
2. Determine Your Purpose 78
   - The Purpose Journey 82
   - Guide to Writing Your Purpose Statement................................. 84
   - My Life Purpose Statement 84
3. Explore Your Behavior, Values and Beliefs................................... 85
   - Behavior Observations... 88
   - Values Observations 89
   - Beliefs Observations 90
4. Confirm Your Passion.. 94
   - Encore Leadership Mindset Shifts 98
   - ReCareer Assessment Observations... 100
   - Hardy Personality Index Observations..................................... 101
   - Passion Defined... 102
5. Proclaim Your Vision... 103
   - Vision Worksheet 107
   - Maxwell Vision THINKing.. 108
   - Your Vision Statement... 109
6. Design Your Personal Strategic Plan... 110
   - Personal Strategic Visioning... 113
   - Personal Strategic Visioning Worksheet 116
   - Blair GOALS Questions 118
   - Gordon SUCCESS Questions.. 119

7. Inventory Your Assets 120
   Life Options® Assessment 123
   ReCareer Results 125
   Time Assessment Results 126
   Just Say NO 127
   Treasure 128
8. Build Your Network 129
   Elevator Speech 132
   Walker-Robertson Networking Tips 133
   Circles of Influence 134
   Board of Advisors 136
   Endorsement 138
9. Brand Your Identity 139
   Clarke's Personal Brand Model 142
   Brand Coaching Questions 143
   Samuel's Branding Checklist 144
   Social Media Optimization 145
10. Execute Your Plan 147
    Comfort Zone 150
    THINK 151
    25 Things to Do NOW 153
11. Evaluate Your Journey 154
    Evaluate Your Transformation 157
    Repacked Bag 158
12. Innovate and Reinvent 159

SECTION IV: GETTING STARTED 165

10 Steps to Get You Started 167
Encore Leadership Dashboard 168
Encore Leadership Assessments 170

The Coach Approach 171
    Coaching "It" 172
    Coaching Personal Profile 173
    10 Goals to Reach in the Next 90 Days 178
    Coaching Session Preparation Form 179
    Coaching Conversation 180
Encore Leadership Communities of Engagement 181
Stay Connected… 182
Recommended Reading and Resources 183
Acknowledgments 188
About the Author 189
About Crystal Stairs, Inc. 190

Introduction

Encore Leaders are successful people who are engaging in legacy work that matters!

If you are...

- an empty nester wanting to continue to support the development of young people;
- a retired executive or graduated corporate leader considering the next phase of your life;
- a teacher shifting from teaching in the classroom to impacting educational systems in communities;
- a successful professional seeking ways to focus on your passion;
- a person concerned about doing work that will make a difference in the world — now and in the future;
- waiting to share your story or expertise in a book;
- ready to define your own destiny as opposed to allowing others to shut down your dreams and aspirations;
- bored with your current way of doing and being and you seek new ways of acting and mattering in various communities of engagement;
- wondering if your time, talent and treasure are being utilized in ways that really matter to you;
- THINKing about the next chapter, second act, second half, halftime, re-invention, or a re-imagined existence...

Then...

The *Encore Leadership* book series and our coaching services — combined with our facilitation tools — will guide you in building a transition roadmap to contemplate and act upon the shifts and the changes that are necessary to achieve alignment and greater success.

This workbook is intended for your personal documentation of your Encore Leadership journey. Write in it. Scribble notes. Jot down insights. Document 'ah-ha' moments. Keep a summary of your assessment findings. It is our hope that this companion workbook, along with the process book and journal, will organize your THINKing into a pathway for greater success and, ultimately, a significant legacy that matters.

SECTION I:

PERSONAL REFLECTION

SECTION I

Tools for Reflection

This section of the *Encore Leadership Workbook* invites you to take the time to THINK about your personal journey. You should complete the exercises offered in this book when you have had the time to reflect upon your responses. Then, document the shifts that you will need to make in order to continue your transition journey.

The tools in this section include:

1. Situations
2. Quality of Life 100™
3. From Sick and Tired to Strong and Tenacious
4. Goals Inventory

SITUATIONS

To prepare for your transition journey to transform your time, talent and treasure, please take a moment to reflect upon the situations that have led you to this moment in your life. These notes will help you begin to THINK about where you've successfully navigated from as you position your future destination. What are five situations that resonate as contributing to your desire and/or need to shift?

THINKing about situation #1: _____

_____
_____
_____
_____
_____
_____
_____
_____
_____
_____
_____
_____
_____
_____
_____
_____
_____
_____
_____

THINKing about situation #2: _____

_____
_____
_____
_____
_____
_____
_____
_____
_____
_____
_____
_____
_____
_____
_____
_____
_____
_____
_____

THINKing about situation #3: _____

___

SECTION 1: PERSONAL REFLECTION

THINKing about situation #4:

THINKing about situation #5: _____

_____
_____
_____
_____
_____
_____
_____
_____
_____
_____
_____
_____
_____
_____
_____
_____
_____
_____

SECTION 1: PERSONAL REFLECTION

QUALITY OF LIFE 100™

Instructions

1. Check the box if the statement is consistently true for you.
2. If the statement doesn't apply to you, please change it so that it does, or replace it with a different one that fits within that category.
3. Add up your section and total scores.
4. Check back every 30 or 90 days and you will likely see progress, even if you aren't focusing directly on this program.
5. Work with a coach or mentor to help you get through the challenging items.

FAMILY AND RELATIONSHIPS

☐ 1. I am both pleased and content with my spouse/partner, or happy being single.
☐ 2. I am close to my parent(s) alive or not. There is nothing in the way. Nothing between us.
☐ 3. I have a circle of friends who I truly enjoy, without any effort
☐ 4. I have a best friend and treat him/her extremely well.
☐ 5. I am very close to my children. There is nothing in the way.
☐ 6. I enjoy my family/extended family; we have worked through any dysfunction and past problems.
☐ 7. I am part of a professional network that stimulates me intellectually and emotionally.
☐ 8. I get along well with my neighbors.
☐ 9. I have at least 20 friends and colleagues who live outside my country of residence.
☐ 10. I am loved by the people who man the most to me.

_____Section Score (Number of checked boxes)

SECTION 1: PERSONAL REFLECTION

CAREER AND BUSINESS

- ☐ 11. My work/career is both fulfilling and nourishing to me; I am not drained
- ☐ 12. I am highly regarded for my expertise by my manager, clients and/or colleagues.
- ☐ 13. I am on a positive career path that leads to increased opportunities and raises.
- ☐ 14. I work in the right industry or field; t has a bright future
- ☐ 15. I look forward to going to work virtually every day.
- ☐ 16. My work is not my life, but it is a rich part of my life.
- ☐ 17. I work with the right people.
- ☐ 18. My work environment brings out the very best of me because it is wonderfully stimulating and /or very supportive.
- ☐ 19. At the end of the day, I have as much energy as I did when I started the day. I am not drained
- ☐ 20. The work I do helps to meet my intellectual, social and /or emotional needs.

_____ Section Score (Number of checked boxes)

MONEY AND FINANCES

- ☐ 21. I have at least a year's living expenses in the bank or money market fund.
- ☐ 22. I am on a financial independence track or am already there.
- ☐ 23. I don't have to work at financial success; money seems to find me with very little effort or pushing.
- ☐ 24. I have no financial stress of any kind in my life.
- ☐ 25. I invest at least 10% of my income/earnings in my ability to increase/expand that income.
- ☐ 26. I do not carry credit card debt; I do not overspend.
- ☐ 27. When I buy something, I buy the best possible quality.
- ☐ 28. I don't lose sleep over my investments.
- ☐ 29. I am financially knowledgeable – I know how money is made and lost.
- ☐ 30. I make money because I provide more than enough value to the people/customers who need what I have.

_____ Section Score (Number of checked boxes)

SECTION 1: PERSONAL REFLECTION

JOY AND DELIGHT

- ☐ 31. I spend my leisure time totally enjoying my interests. I am never bored.
- ☐ 32. Weekends (or others days off) are a joy for me.
- ☐ 33. I have designed the perfect way to spend the last hour of my day.
- ☐ 34. I look forward to getting up virtually every morning.
- ☐ 35. I am very, very happy.
- ☐ 36. I have designed – and am living – the perfect lifestyle for me right now.
- ☐ 37. I have at least an hour a day that is exclusively for me and I spend it in a chosen way.
- ☐ 38. I am able to stay present during the day; I don't lose myself to stress or adrenaline.
- ☐ 39. I easily take delight in the smallest things.
- ☐ 40. My home brings me joy every time I walk inside.

_____ *Section Score (Number of checked boxes)*

EFFECTIVENESS AND EFFICIENCY

- ☐ 41. I don't spend time with anyone who bugs me or who is using me.
- ☐ 42. I have more than enough energy and vitality to get me through the day; I don't start dragging.
- ☐ 43. I have no problem asking for exactly what I want, from anyone.
- ☐ 44. I have all of the right tools, equipment, computers, software and peripherals that I need to work well.
- ☐ 45. Whatever can be automated, is automated.
- ☐ 46. Whatever can be delegated, is delegated.
- ☐ 47. I reply to all emails as I read them; I don't maintain an inventory of unanswered emails.
- ☐ 48. I don't put things off; when it occurs to me, I do it, handle it or have it done.
- ☐ 49. I know what my goals are and I am eagerly and effectively making them a reality.
- ☐ 50. I don't do errands, except by exception.

_____ *Section Score (Number of checked boxes)*

SECTION 1: PERSONAL REFLECTION

RESPONSIBILITY AND FOUNDATION

- [ ] 51. I love my home: Its location, style, furnishings, light, feeling.
- [ ] 52. My boundaries are strong enough that people respect me, my needs and what I want.
- [ ] 53. I tolerate very, very little; I'm just not willing to.
- [ ] 54. I don't see a cloud on my future's horizon; it looks clear.
- [ ] 55. My wants have been satisfied; there is little I want.
- [ ] 56. My personal needs have been satisfied; I am not driven or motivated by unmet needs.
- [ ] 57. There is nothing I am dreading or avoiding.
- [ ] 58. My personal values are clear; I am oriented around them.
- [ ] 59. I have resolved the stresses and key issues of my upbringing and past events.
- [ ] 60. I don't have a lot of unfinished projects, business or hanging items; I am caught up.

_____Section score (Number of checked boxes)

PERSONAL DEVELOPMENT AND EVOLUTION

- [ ] 61. I could die this afternoon with no regrets.
- [ ] 62. I am living my life, not the life that someone else designed for me or expected of me.
- [ ] 63. There is nothing that I am not facing head-on; nothing that I am putting off dealing with.
- [ ] 64. I attract success; I don't have to strive for it or chase it.
- [ ] 65. I have more than enough natural motivation, inspiration and synergy in my life; I am not stuck.
- [ ] 66. I am evolving, not just improving, because I continually experiment.
- [ ] 67. I have progressed beyond the notion of beliefs.
- [ ] 68. I am at that place in life where I initiate and cause events, not wait for others or events to do so.
- [ ] 69. I have learned to take the path of least resistance as I accomplish my goals.
- [ ] 70. I am beyond striving for success; simply enjoy my life and focus on what fulfills me.

_____Section Score (Number of checked boxes)

SECTION 1: PERSONAL REFLECTION

SELF-CARE AND VITALITY

- ☐ 71. I take at least 4 vacations a year.
- ☐ 72. Life is easy; I have virtually no problems or unresolved matters affecting me.
- ☐ 73. My teeth and gums look great and are in top condition.
- ☐ 74. I have more than enough time during my day.
- ☐ 75. I eat food for sustenance and pleasure, not for emotional comfort.
- ☐ 76. I am not abusing my body with too much alcohol, television, caffeine or drugs.
- ☐ 77. Whatever health problems I have, I am receiving proper, effective care for them.
- ☐ 78. My body is in great shape.
- ☐ 79. I reduce stress daily by meditating, taking a long bath, exercising, walking etc.
- ☐ 80. There is nothing I am doing that is messing up my mind or heart.

_____ Section Score (Number of checked boxes)

HAPPINESS AND CONTENTMENT

Please write down 10 situations, routines or scenarios that make, or would make, you the happiest and most content.

- ☐ 81. Situation #1 _____
- ☐ 82. Situation #2 _____
- ☐ 83. Situation #3 _____
- ☐ 84. Situation #4 _____
- ☐ 85. Situation #5 _____
- ☐ 86. Situation #6 _____
- ☐ 87. Situation #7 _____
- ☐ 88. Situation #8 _____
- ☐ 89. Situation #9 _____
- ☐ 90. Situation #10 _____

_____ Section Score (Number of checked boxes)

PLEASURE AND EXCITEMENT

Please write down 10 activities that you truly enjoy, whether you currently do these things in your life or not.

- ☐ 91. Activity #1 _____
- ☐ 92. Activity #2 _____
- ☐ 93. Activity #3 _____
- ☐ 94. Activity #4 _____
- ☐ 95. Activity #5 _____
- ☐ 96. Activity #6 _____
- ☐ 97. Activity #7 _____
- ☐ 98. Activity #8 _____
- ☐ 99. Activity #9 _____
- ☐ 100. Activity #10 _____

_____ Section Score (Number of checked boxes)

_____ **TOTAL SCORE (Number of checked boxes)**

SCORING KEY

90-100	Awesome. Congratulations. Incredible.
80-89	Excellent! Your score is very high – this is a tough test.
70-79	Very good. You're definitely on the right track. Keep going.
60-69	Pretty good, but there is some work to do.
50-59	Average score. Why not make your quality of life a priority and score 10 more points in the next month?
40-49	You may need to make some important changes.
30-39	Weak. What's up with this? Make yourself a priority!
00-29	Hello? Anybody home?

V1.1 ©2000 by Thomas J. Leonard. Duplication, with attribution, permitted and encouraged.

FROM SICK AND TIRED TO STRONG AND TENACIOUS

We often utter the words that we are "sick and tired" of something, but we seldom consciously and intentionally decide to shift our behavior so that we become "strong and tenacious" about moving forward. Take the time to identify the top seven things that you are "sick and tired" of tolerating that are impacting your ability to achieve your goals.

SICK and TIRED
1.
2.
3.
4.
5.
6.
7.

SECTION 1: PERSONAL REFLECTION

Now, focus on the seven items that you are sick and tired of tolerating and THINK about how you can begin to make the shifts necessary to change your landscape of toleration.

STRONG and TENACIOUS
1.
2.
3.
4.
5.
6.
7.

What insight did you gain from focusing on being "sick and tired" and shifting to "strong and tenacious"? _____

_____

_____

_____

_____

_____

_____

_____

_____

_____

_____

_____

_____

_____

_____

_____

_____

GOALS INVENTORY

Clarity on the goals that are important to achieve as a component of your Encore Leadership journey is extremely helpful. Take a few moments to document your goals inventory utilizing the Crystal Stairs Life Compass categories as a starting point. Highlight 3 top focus items on the inventory. (Refer to process book, pages 81.)

CATEGORY	MAJOR GOALS	CURRENT STATE (1-5)	POTENTIAL IMPACT (1-5)	FOCUS
FAMILY	1. 2. 3.			
FRIENDS	1. 2. 3.			
NETWORK	1. 2. 3.			
SOCIAL/RELATION-SHIPS	1. 2. 3.			
PROFESSION	1. 2. 3.			

SECTION 1: PERSONAL REFLECTION

INTELLECT	1. 2. 3.			
SPIRITUAL	1. 2. 3.			
ENVIRONMENT	1. 2. 3.			
HEALTH	1. 2. 3.			
FINANCIAL	1. 2. 3.			
HOBBIES/FUN	1. 2. 3.			
EXTREME SELF-CARE	1. 2. 3.			
OTHER	1. 2. 3.			

SECTION 1: PERSONAL REFLECTION

SECTION II:

PREPARING FOR THE TRANSFORMATION JOURNEY

SECTION II

Exercises to Help You Shift on Your Journey

This section of the *Encore Leadership Workbook* challenges you to THINK about the shifts required that will help you on your transformation journey. You should complete the exercises offered in this book when you have had the time to reflect upon your responses. Then, document the shifts that you will need to make in order to continue your transition journey.

The tools in this section include:

1. Sheroes and Heroes
2. Encore Leadership Skill Set
3. Skills Renewal
4. Halftime
5. The Story of Your Life
6. The "Good Life Inventory"
7. Visioning of Future Self

SHEROES AND HEROES

List the names of 5 individuals who have impacted your life. Write a succinct statement of the impact each has had.

NAME	IMPACT
1.	
2.	
3.	
4.	
5.	

Write down the 3 names in the sections below and write an appreciation and/or gratitude letter to 3 of the 5 individuals.

THINK about individual #1: _____

_____
_____
_____
_____
_____
_____
_____
_____
_____
_____
_____
_____
_____
_____

SECTION II: PREPARING FOR THE TRANSFORMATION JOURNEY

THINK about individual #2: _____

THINK about individual #3: _____

ENCORE LEADERSHIP ATTRIBUTES

The attributes in the Transition Competency Optimization Model©, which follows, were determined to be critical readiness elements by transitioning executives. Assess your current readiness on a scale of 1-5, with 5 being READY. The exercises "Attributes to Reframe your Life" and "Attributes to Renew your Life" will help you to gain insight of the areas in which you need to focus as you transform your life. (Refer to process book, pages 25 – 36.)

RECOMMENDED READING

Foster, J. M. (2009). Cracking the Transition Code: A Paradigmatic Framework of Competencies that Construct the Reality of 50+ Black Executive Transitions. *Dissertation, 267 (UMI No. 3367130).*

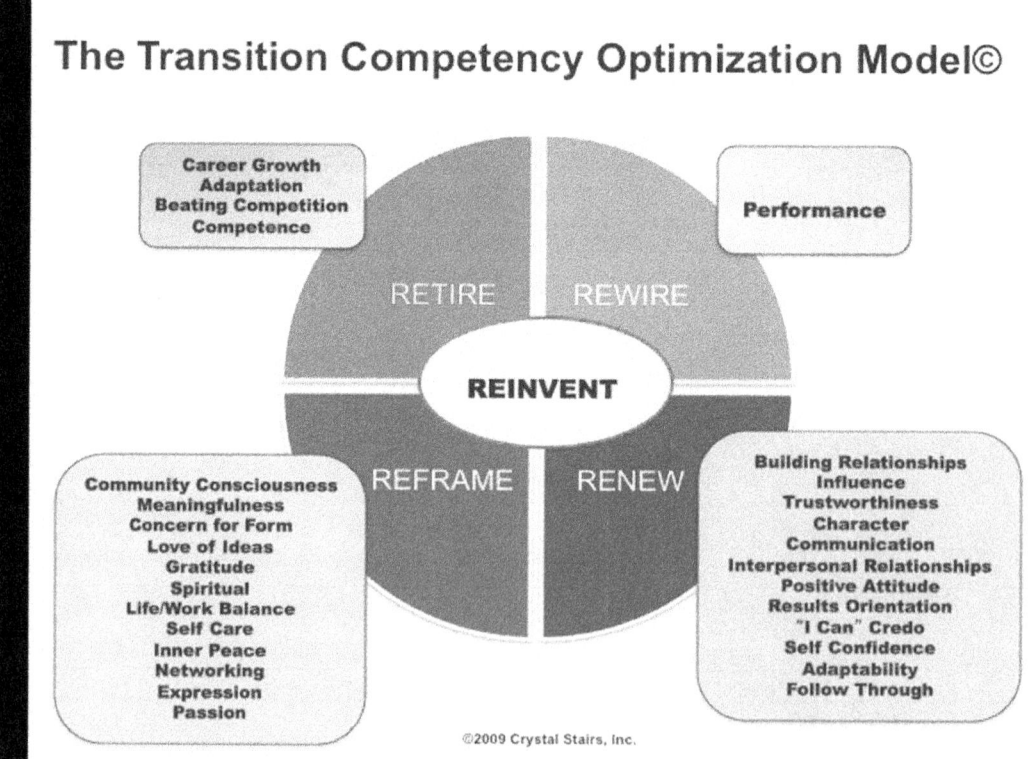

ATTRIBUTES TO REFRAME YOUR LIFE

Attribute	1	2	3	4	5	Focus
Community Consciousness						
Meaningfulness						
Concern for Form						
Love of Ideas						
Gratitude						
Spiritual						
Life/Work Balance						
Self Care						
Inner Peace						
Networking						
Expression						
Passion						

Attributes to Focus on:

1. _____

_____

2. _____

_____

3. _____

_____

SECTION II: PREPARING FOR THE TRANSFORMATION JOURNEY

ATTRIBUTES TO RENEW YOUR LIFE

Attribute	1	2	3	4	5	Focus
Building Relationships						
Influence						
Trustworthiness						
Character						
Communication						
Interpersonal Relationships						
Positive Attitude						
Results Orientation						
"I Can" Credo						
Self Confidence						
Adaptability						
Follow Through						

Attributes to Focus on:

1. _____

   _____

2. _____

   _____

3. _____

   _____

HALFTIME

Document your responses to Bob Buford's "Halftime" Questions. (Refer to process book, page 42.)

> **RECOMMENDED READING**
>
> Buford, B. (2000). *Halftime: Changing Your Life Plan from Success to Significance.* Grand Rapids, MI: Zondervan.

THINK and reply to question #1: _____

_____

_____

_____

THINK and reply to question #2: _____

_____

_____

_____

THINK and reply to question #3: _____

_____

_____

_____

THINK and reply to question #4: _____

_____

_____

_____

SECTION II: PREPARING FOR THE TRANSFORMATION JOURNEY

THINK and reply to question #5: _____

_____

_____

_____

THINK and reply to question #6: _____

_____

_____

_____

THINK and reply to question #7: _____

_____

_____

_____

THINK and reply to question #8: _____

_____

_____

_____

THINK and reply to question #9: _____

_____

_____

_____

_____

_____

_____

THINK and reply to question #10: _____

_____

_____

_____

_____

_____

_____

_____

SECTION II: PREPARING FOR THE TRANSFORMATION JOURNEY

THE GOOD LIFE INVENTORY

The Inventure Group defines and assesses the "Good Life" through an inventory of key characteristics of people who are living the "Good Life." The Group offers a provocative opportunity to explore your thoughts relative to the status of your "Good Life." Share your insight from this assessment, which you can obtain at www.InventureGroup.com. (Refer to process book, pages 55 and 56.)

RECOMMENDED READING

Leider, R. J., & Shapiro, D. A. (2012). *Repacking Your Bags: Lighten Your Load For the Good Life.* San Francisco, CA: Berrett-Koehler Publishers, Inc.

FOCUS: _____

_____

_____

_____

_____

_____

_____

_____

_____

_____

CHALLENGES: _____

ACTION: _____

THE STORY OF YOUR LIFE

One of the most challenging but liberating exercises in which you can engage is to write down the story of your life. Some individuals take the opportunity to do this through recalling and writing about key moments in life. Others often write their obituary, concluding with "wishes" for their family. Whatever sparks your creative energy to write down your life's story, use that inspiration to record your story on the following pages of this workbook. (Refer to process book, pages 57 and 58.)

> **RECOMMENDED READING**
>
> Loehr, J. (2007). *The Power of Story: Change your story, change your destiny in business and in life.* New York, NY: Simon & Schuster, Inc.

SECTION II: PREPARING FOR THE TRANSFORMATION JOURNEY

SECTION II: PREPARING FOR THE TRANSFORMATION JOURNEY

SECTION II: PREPARING FOR THE TRANSFORMATION JOURNEY

SECTION II: PREPARING FOR THE TRANSFORMATION JOURNEY

VISIONING OF FUTURE SELF

Continue to gain clarity as you transform your time, talent and treasure into a legacy that matters. Consider and document responses to the following questions:

What will your Legacy consist of? _____

_____

_____

_____

_____

What would a significant person in your life say about you? _____

_____

_____

_____

_____

When you THINK about your past, what woke up your energy? _____

_____

_____

_____

_____

What current issues and/or challenges are you passionate about helping to solve?

_____
_____
_____
_____
_____
_____
_____

What dreams are on the back burner of your current life that you need to switch on?

_____
_____
_____
_____
_____
_____
_____

What do others say you're good at? _____

_____

_____

_____

_____

_____

_____

What will you be doing next year that is different from what you are doing now?

_____

_____

_____

_____

_____

_____

What is the BIG STEP you will take to shift your life NOW? _____

_____
_____
_____
_____
_____
_____
_____

What will you be doing in 5 years? _____

_____
_____
_____
_____
_____
_____
_____

Who will you engage as your accountability partner to share this journey of transformation with you? _____

_____

_____

_____

_____

_____

_____

When will you schedule your accountability sessions? _____

_____

_____

_____

_____

_____

_____

SECTION III:

THE ENCORE LEADERSHIP PROCESS©

SECTION III

4 Stages, 12 Steps

The Encore Leadership Process begins with a ***Transition Tipping Point***. You then engage through four stages of shifting — driven by 12 steps.

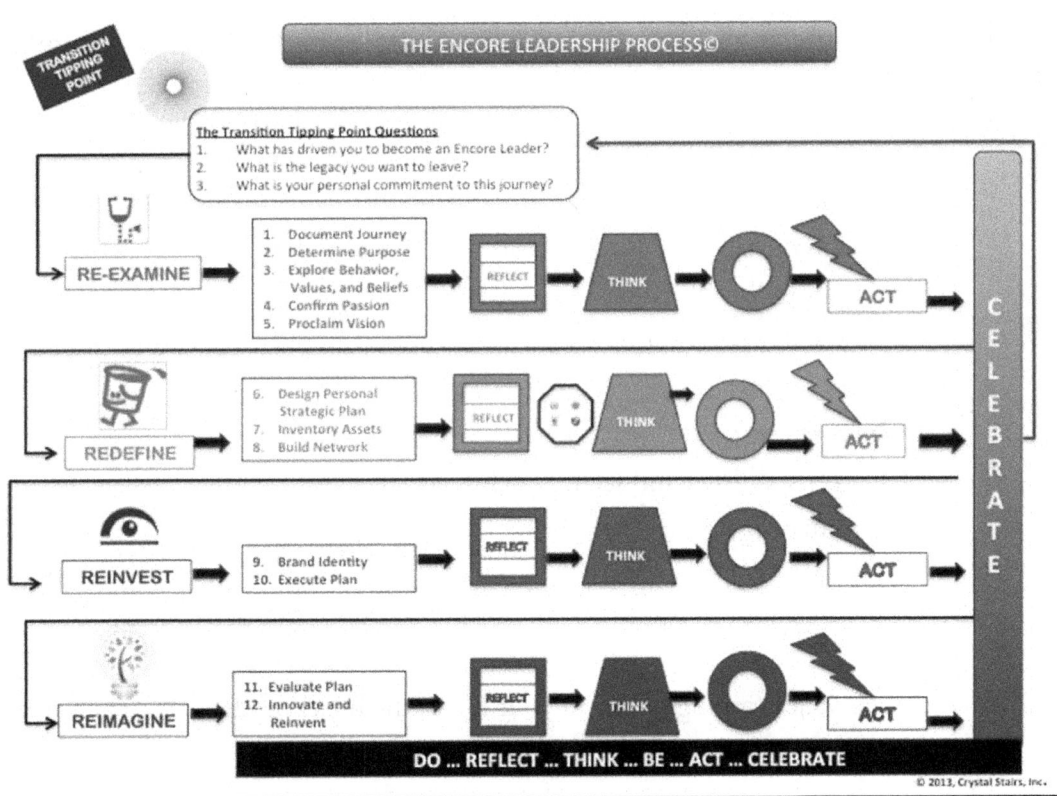

THE TRANSITION TIPPING POINT

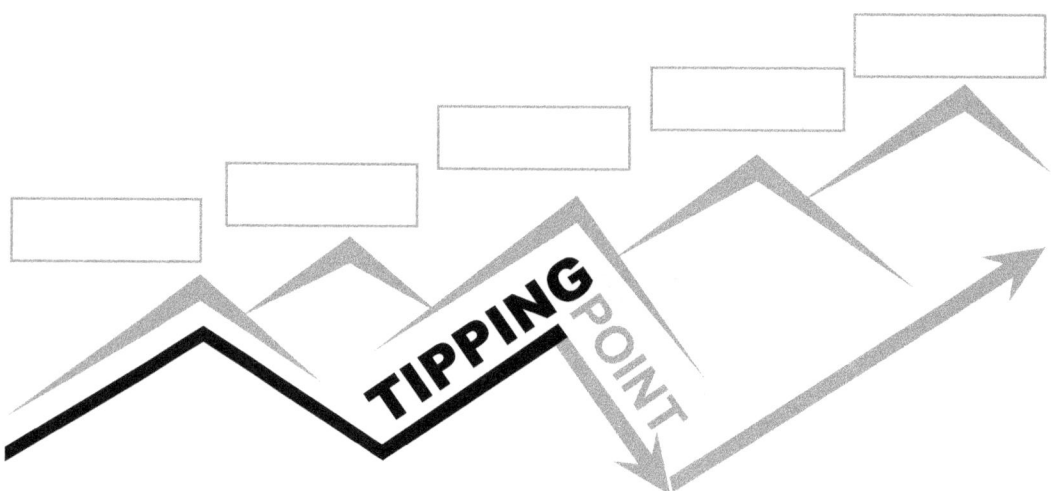

THINK about the situations that have placed you at a *Transition Tipping Point*. Did the situation cause you to consider a shift or a change in the direction of your life? Encore Leadership research has identified the following THINKing triggers: (Refer to process book, pages 17–23.)

- Change in environment
- Political shift
- Economic shift
- Organization climate
- Personal matters
- New opportunity
- Non-voluntary
- Career stabilized and security achieved
- Spiritual
- Dreams
- Personal realization

Write down five major tipping points in your life in the boxes on the diagram above.

SECTION III: THE ENCORE LEADERSHIP PROCESS©

Often, the ***Transition Tipping Point*** is observed when the following conditions occur and/or environments shift:

- Empty nest
- Job transition
- Retirement
- Boredom
- Desire to make a greater contribution
- Change in profession
- Tragedy that invokes greater desire for achievement
- The continuous "What's Next?" question

Write a story about your ***Transition Tipping Points***. _____

_____

_____

_____

_____

_____

_____

_____

_____

SECTION III: THE ENCORE LEADERSHIP PROCESS©

SECTION III: THE ENCORE LEADERSHIP PROCESS©

POIGNANT, PROVOCATIVE AND PIVOTAL QUESTIONS

Questions that shift your THINKing are critical as you travel on your transformation journey. Reflect upon these questions and document your THINKing. (Refer to process book, page 59.)

What's next? _____

_____

_____

_____

_____

What's your definition of "The Good Life"? _____

_____

_____

_____

_____

Are you living your "Good Life"? _____

_____

_____

_____

SECTION III: THE ENCORE LEADERSHIP PROCESS©

What needs to change or shift? _____

_____

_____

_____

_____

What is the meaning of your life? _____

_____

_____

_____

_____

What keeps you up at night vs. what wakes you up in the morning? _____

_____

_____

_____

_____

_____

_____

_____

What are your life's non-negotiables? _____

_____

_____

_____

_____

How much is enough? _____

_____

_____

_____

_____

What do you really want to carry on the next phase of your journey? _____

_____

_____

_____

_____

_____

_____

Does all this make you happy? _____

_____

_____

_____

_____

Where do you go for solitude? _____

_____

_____

_____

_____

What are the lengths of time you engage in solitude? _____

_____

_____

_____

_____

_____

Are you living in your own big questions? _____

_____

_____

_____

_____

_____

YOUR BIG QUESTION? _____

_____

_____

_____

_____

_____

YOUR NEXT QUESTION? _____

_____

_____

_____

_____

_____

ENCORE LEADERSHIP MINDSET

Developing an appropriate mindset is critical to a successful transformation as an Encore Leader. In the chart that follows, describe your current state, your desired future state, and the actions you plan to take to achieve the desired state. (Refer to process book, pages 45–56.)

> **RECOMMENDED READING**
> Shickler, S. & Waller, J. (2011). *The 7 Mindsets To Live Your Ultimate Life.* Roswell, GA: Ultimate Life Media, a division of Excent Corporation.

Having "An Attitude of Gratitude"		
Current State	Desired Future State	Actions
Striving for Success and Significance		
Current State	Desired Future State	Actions

SECTION III: THE ENCORE LEADERSHIP PROCESS©

Sharing Wisdom

Current State	Desired Future State	Actions

Mattering

Current State	Desired Future State	Actions

Appreciating Solitude

Current State	Desired Future State	Actions

Knowing your "Good Life"

Current State	Desired Future State	Actions

Valuing the Freedom to Choose

Current State	Desired Future State	Actions

Three key actions to take immediately to shift your *Encore Leadership Mindset*

1. _____

_____

_____

_____

_____

2. _____

_____

_____

_____

_____

_____

_____

3. _____

_____

_____

_____

_____

_____

_____

SECTION III

The 12 Steps of Transformation

Each of the 12 steps will represent a phase in the process of transforming your time, talent and treasure into a legacy that matters. The 12 steps are:

1. Document your journey
2. Determine your purpose
3. Explore your behavior, values and beliefs
4. Confirm your passion
5. Proclaim your vision
6. Design your personal strategic plan
7. Inventory your assets
8. Build your network
9. Brand your identity
10. Execute your plan
11. Evaluate your journey
12. Innovate and reinvent

THE ENCORE LEADERSHIP PROCESS©
12 STEPS

Phase 1

1. Document your journey
2. Determine your purpose
3. Explore your behavior, values and beliefs
4. Confirm your passion
5. Proclaim your vision

Phase 2

6. Design your personal strategic plan
7. Inventory your assets
8. Build your network

Phase 3

9. Brand your identity
10. Execute your plan

Phase 4

11. Evaluate your journey
12. Innovate and Reinvent

1. DOCUMENT YOUR JOURNEY

Step 1 document journey—INSIGHT: _____

_____

_____

Step 2 determine purpose—INSIGHT: _____

_____

_____

Step 3 explore BV&Bs—INSIGHT: _____

_____

_____

Step 4 confirm passion—INSIGHT: _____

_____

_____

_____

Step 5 proclaim vision—INSIGHT: _____

_____

_____

Step 6 design strategic plan—INSIGHT: _____

_____

_____

Step 7 inventory assets—INSIGHT: _____

_____

_____

Step 8 build network—INSIGHT: _____

_____

_____

SECTION III: THE ENCORE LEADERSHIP PROCESS©

Step 9 brand identity—INSIGHT: _____

_____

_____

Step 10 execute plan—INSIGHT: _____

_____

_____

Step 11 evaluate journey—INSIGHT: _____

_____

_____

_____

Step 12 innovate/reinvent—INSIGHT: _____

_____

_____

_____

SECTION III: THE ENCORE LEADERSHIP PROCESS©

THE TRANSITION JOURNEY EXERCISE

The "Transition Journey" exercise was created as a means to plot past successes, to highlight current areas of focus, and to begin to THINK about "what's next?" Taking the time to then look at the story that is told by the chart provides an initial roadmap to reflect upon the journey.

Reinforcing the work associated with the past drives the need to ask the question, "Have I accomplished what I was placed on this earth to do?" What other questions does this exercise inspire?

Please complete the following steps to begin the journey:

1. **Establish the age boundaries to look at the Legacy Gap**
    a. Draw a vertical line from your current age
    b. Draw a vertical line at where you forecast your life's journey will conclude
    c. Draw a horizontal line to indicate the amount of time to think about for developing your goals and objectives
    d. Write a statement in the legacy space as to how your life will be remembered by others

2. **Work Gap**
    a. Draw a vertical line at the age when you started your professional work life
    b. Draw another line when you plan to no longer work
    c. Draw a horizontal line to think about your view of work from current age to ending work life

3. **List between 1 and 10 major goals that you want to achieve as you contemplate what your life's work will be; THINK about the following categories**
    a. Service to humankind
    b. Passions and hobby
    c. Personal commitments to engage in the world
    d. Organizations where you spend time, energy and resources
    e. A political, spiritual or social challenge that you want to achieve

4. **List your work life goals; THINK about the following categories**
   a. Consider movement within your current job and/or career
   b. Entrepreneurial interests
   c. Shift in industry, geography, functional area
   d. Execute a professional development plan and obtain new skills

5. **Document from 1 to 10 significant events that will occur in your life**
   a. Relationships and Family
   b. Community, Organizations
   c. Personal Goal (Weight, Exercise, Health, etc.)

6. **Seriously reflect on the picture and develop your story**
   a. Establish priorities
   b. Revisit the chart on a regular basis by placing it in your control book

Please refer to the worksheet on the two pages that follow when completing steps 1–6 of *The Transition Journey Exercise*.

TRANSITION JOURNEY

NAME _____

LEGACY:

	age	0-9	10-19	20-29
LIFE WORK ☐ LW1 ☐ LW2 ☐ LW3 ☐ LW4 ☐ LW5 ☐ LW6 ☐ LW7 ☐ LW8 ☐ LW9 ☐ LW10				
WORK LIFE ☐ WL1 ☐ WL2 ☐ WL3 ☐ WL4 ☐ WL5 ☐ WL6 ☐ WL7 ☐ WL8 ☐ WL9 ☐ WL10				
SIGNIFICANT EVENTS ☐ SE1 ☐ SE2 ☐ SE3 ☐ SE4 ☐ SE5 ☐ SE6 ☐ SE7 ☐ SE8 ☐ SE9 ☐ SE10				
		0		25
		Yr Born ←		

Draw Vertical lines at the following years
Legacy Gap: Draw Horizontal Line Between Current Age and Life Expectancy;
Reveals time available to leave a legacy

SECTION III: THE ENCORE LEADERSHIP PROCESS©

Transforming Time, Talent and Treasure Into a Legacy that Matters **73**

WORKSHEET

DATE _____

30-39	40-49	50-59	60-69	70-79	80-89	90-99

		50		75		100
Current Age		→				Life Expectancy

Work Gap: Draw Horizontal Line between Start Date and End Date; Shows work life progression

2006 Crystal Stairs, Inc.

SECTION III: THE ENCORE LEADERSHIP PROCESS©

THE BIG 5 GAME CHANGERS

Describe the past, present and future experiences that you would consider game changers. (Refer to process book, pages 56 and 57.)

Past Experiences	
1.	
2.	
3.	
4.	
5.	

Present Experiences	
1.	
2.	
3.	
4.	
5.	

Future Experiences Planned
1.
2.
3.
4.
5.

SECTION III: THE ENCORE LEADERSHIP PROCESS©

LIFELINE EXERCISE

Map the storyboard of your life into blocks in the chart that follows. From each of the key blocks of your life, create a PowerPoint slide. Present the PowerPoint lifeline to your family, friends or an organization where you hold a membership to connect with peers who would be interested in knowing more about you. (Refer to process book, page 68.)

BUCKET LIST

Think about the things that you have always wanted to do in life. Document a list of the top 10 "to-dos" in the Black, Medium Grey or Light Grey Buckets that follow. As you progress from Light Grey (bottom) to Black (top), the importance of achieving "to-dos" increases. Make a plan to execute at least one "to-do" in the Light Grey bucket within the next year. (Refer to process book, pages 68 and 69.)

SECTION III: THE ENCORE LEADERSHIP PROCESS©

2. DETERMINE YOUR PURPOSE

Step 1 document journey—INSIGHT: _____

_____

_____

_____

_____

Step 2 determine purpose—INSIGHT: _____

_____

_____

_____

_____

Step 3 explore BV&Bs—INSIGHT: _____

_____

_____

_____

_____

Step 4 confirm passion—INSIGHT: _____

_____
_____
_____
_____

Step 5 proclaim vision—INSIGHT: _____

_____
_____
_____
_____

Step 6 design strategic plan—INSIGHT: _____

_____
_____
_____
_____
_____

Step 7 inventory assets—INSIGHT: _____

_____

_____

_____

_____

Step 8 build network—INSIGHT: _____

_____

_____

_____

_____

Step 9 brand identity—INSIGHT: _____

_____

_____

_____

_____

Step 10 execute plan—INSIGHT: _____

_____
_____
_____
_____
_____

Step 11 evaluate journey—INSIGHT: _____

_____
_____
_____
_____
_____

Step 12 innovate/reinvent—INSIGHT: _____

_____
_____
_____
_____
_____

THE PURPOSE JOURNEY

Stages of Life (Age)	Purpose	Measure of Success
0–5		
6–12		
13–18		
19–26		
27–37		

38–48		
49–59		
60–69		
70–79		
80–89		
90+		

GUIDE TO WRITING YOUR PURPOSE STATEMENT

Richard Leider shares a guide about how to write your purpose statement that I found helpful. What are your observations of the guide? Write down your thoughts in the spaces that follow.

Order from the store at www.InventureGroup.com: *Putting Purpose to Work Guide.*

MY LIFE PURPOSE STATEMENT

3. EXPLORE YOUR BEHAVIOR, VALUES AND BELIEFS

Step 1 document journey—INSIGHT: _____

_____

_____

_____

Step 2 determine purpose—INSIGHT: _____

_____

_____

_____

Step 3 explore BV&Bs—INSIGHT: _____

_____

_____

_____

Step 4 confirm passion—INSIGHT: _____

_____

_____

_____

Step 5 proclaim vision—INSIGHT: _____

_____

_____

Step 6 design strategic plan—INSIGHT: _____

_____

_____

Step 7 inventory assets—INSIGHT: _____

_____

_____

Step 8 build network—INSIGHT: _____

_____

_____

_____

Step 9 brand identity—INSIGHT: _____

_____

_____

Step 10 execute plan—INSIGHT: _____

_____

_____

Step 11 evaluate journey—INSIGHT: _____

_____

_____

Step 12 innovate/reinvent—INSIGHT: _____

_____

_____

SECTION III: THE ENCORE LEADERSHIP PROCESS©

BEHAVIOR OBSERVATIONS

After you complete work on your behavior style, jot down key take-aways based on the assessment. (Refer to process book, pages 78–80.)

THINK about your behavior style: _____

VALUES OBSERVATIONS

After you complete work on your values, jot down key take-aways based on the assessment. (Refer to process book, pages 81–87.)

> **RECOMMENDED READING**
> Suiter, J. (2003). *Exploring Values! Releasing the power of attitudes.* Peachtree City, GA: Competitive Edge, Inc.

THINK about your values: _____

_____

_____

_____

_____

_____

_____

_____

_____

_____

_____

_____

SECTION III: THE ENCORE LEADERSHIP PROCESS©

BELIEFS OBSERVATIONS

How would you describe your "new normal" as an Encore Leader? (Refer to process book, pages 87–90.)

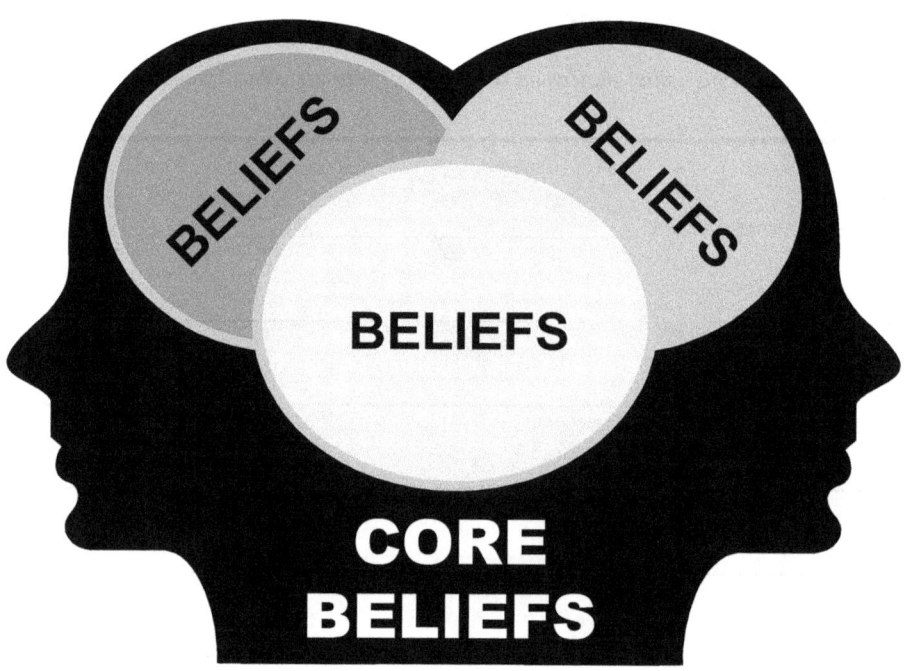

THINK about and describe your "new normal": _____

_____

_____

_____

_____

_____

SECTION III: THE ENCORE LEADERSHIP PROCESS©

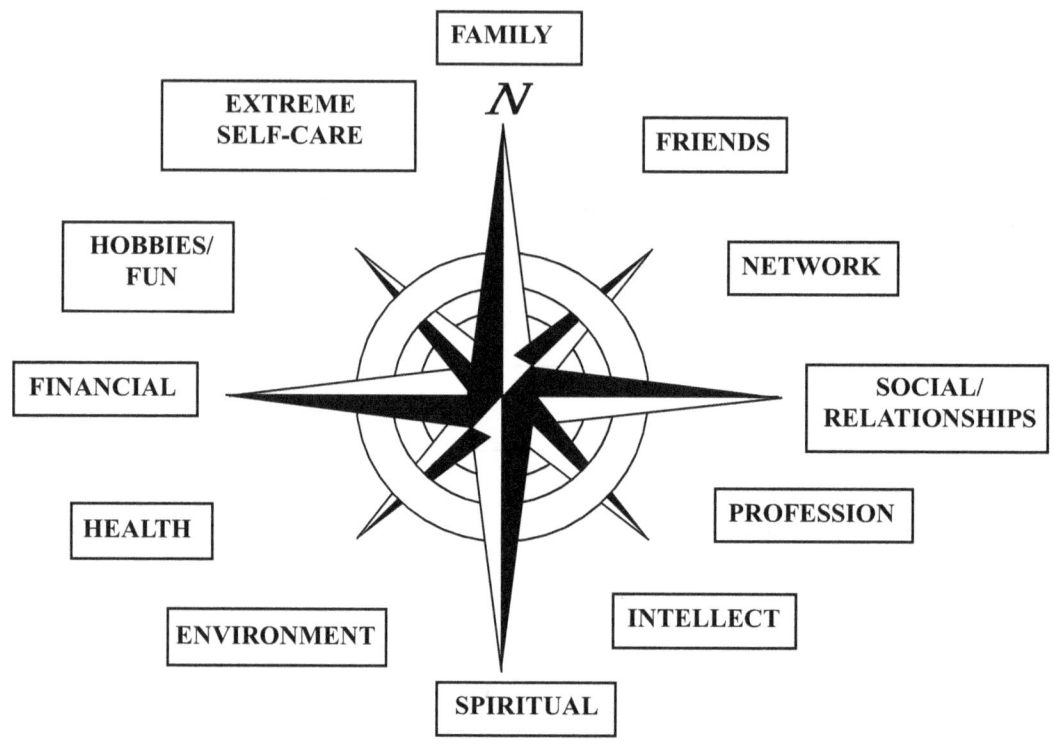

CRYSTAL STAIRS LIFE COMPASS©

A plan to live a meaningful life requires taking a look at where you are today relative to where you want to be in any given aspect of your life.

For each area of your life, assess where you are currently on a scale of 0–10. (0 is the bull's-eye of the circle, no place; 10 is the best it could be, the outer circle perimeter.) Place a dot between 0 and 10 to indicate where you are today. Then connect the dots to find the balance of your compass, your life. Review each and put a dot where you would like to be in the element and connect those dots.

The space in between the dots represents the "gap" that you want to bridge. Prioritize the three largest gaps and take three immediate actions this week to address each of the three. Include a detailed plan as a component of your "journey assessment."

SECTION III: THE ENCORE LEADERSHIP PROCESS©

Large Gap #1: _____

_____

_____

_____

_____

_____

_____

Large Gap #2: _____

_____

_____

_____

_____

_____

_____

Large Gap #3: _____

_____

_____

_____

_____

_____

_____

4. CONFIRM YOUR PASSION

Step 1 document journey—INSIGHT: _____

_____

_____

_____

Step 2 determine purpose—INSIGHT: _____

_____

_____

_____

_____

Step 3 explore BV&Bs—INSIGHT: _____

_____

_____

_____

_____

Step 4 confirm passion—INSIGHT: _____

_____

_____

_____

Step 5 proclaim vision—INSIGHT: _____

_____

_____

_____

Step 6 design strategic plan—INSIGHT: _____

_____

_____

_____

Step 7 inventory assets—INSIGHT: _____

_____

_____

_____

Step 8 build network—INSIGHT: _____

_____

_____

_____

_____

Step 9 brand identity—INSIGHT: _____

_____

_____

_____

_____

Step 10 execute plan—INSIGHT: _____

_____

_____

_____

Step 11 evaluate journey—INSIGHT: _____

_____

_____

_____

_____

Step 12 innovate/reinvent—INSIGHT: _____

_____

_____

_____

_____

ENCORE LEADERSHIP MINDSET SHIFTS

For each of the seven *Encore Leadership Mindsets*, assess your current status and indicate actions that you can take to shift the mindset to a positive mental attitude for transformation. (1 = Needs major work to 5 = Living the mindset)

(Refer to process book, pages 91 and 92.)

Mindset	Current State					Future State					Actions
	1	2	3	4	5	1	2	3	4	5	
Attitude of gratitude											
Strive for significance											
Wisdom sharing											

Work that matters			
Escape for solitude			
Good Life defined			
Freedom to choose			

RECAREER ASSESSMENT OBSERVATIONS

After you complete work on your ReCareer Assessment, jot down key take-aways based on your results. (Refer to process book, page 92.)

> **RECOMMENDED READING**
>
> Johnson Ph.D, R. (2009). *ReCareer, find your authentic work: How to discover and pursue a purposeful ReCareer that stimulates your mind, fires your heart, and feeds your spirit.* St. Louis, MO: Richard P. Johnson.

Results: _____

_____

_____

_____

_____

_____

_____

_____

_____

_____

_____

_____

HARDY PERSONALITY INDEX OBSERVATIONS

After you complete work on your ReCareer Assessment, jot down key take-aways from the Hardy Personality Index, a component of the Assessment. (Refer to process book, page 92.)

Results: _____

_____

_____

_____

_____

_____

_____

_____

_____

_____

_____

_____

_____

_____

PASSION DEFINED

How do you describe your personal passion? _____

5. PROCLAIM YOUR VISION

Step 1 document journey—INSIGHT: _____

_____

_____

_____

_____

Step 2 determine purpose—INSIGHT: _____

_____

_____

_____

_____

Step 3 explore BV&Bs—INSIGHT: _____

_____

_____

_____

_____

Step 4 confirm passion—INSIGHT: _____

_____

_____

_____

_____

Step 5 proclaim vision—INSIGHT: _____

_____

_____

_____

_____

Step 6 design strategic plan—INSIGHT: _____

_____

_____

_____

_____

Step 7 inventory assets—INSIGHT: _____

_____

_____

_____

_____

Step 8 build network—INSIGHT: _____

_____

_____

_____

_____

Step 9 brand identity—INSIGHT: _____

_____

_____

_____

_____

Step 10 execute plan—INSIGHT: _____

_____

_____

_____

_____

Step 11 evaluate journey—INSIGHT: _____

_____

_____

_____

_____

Step 12 innovate/reinvent—INSIGHT: _____

_____

_____

_____

_____

VISION WORKSHEET

How would you like to see the world and your involvement in it during the following time spans?

1 year from now, I envision the world will….   I will take the following actions to help achieve this vision:
5 years from now, I envision the world will….   I will take the following actions to help achieve this vision:
10 years from now, I envision the world will….   I will take the following actions to help achieve this vision:
25 years from now, I envision the world will….   I will take the following actions to help achieve this vision:

SECTION III: THE ENCORE LEADERSHIP PROCESS©

MAXWELL VISION THINKING

Review the six questions that John Maxwell poses to determine your vision. (Refer to process book, page 93.)

> **RECOMMENDED READING**
>
> Maxwell, J. C. (2001). *The Right to Lead: A Study in Character and Courage.* Nashville, TN: J. Countryman®, a division of Thomas Nelson, Inc.

1.

2.

3.

4.

5.

6.

YOUR VISION STATEMENT

Write, draw, doodle, storyboard… your vision.

6. DESIGN YOUR PERSONAL STRATEGIC PLAN

Step 1 document journey—INSIGHT: _____

_____

_____

_____

_____

Step 2 determine purpose—INSIGHT: _____

_____

_____

_____

_____

_____

Step 3 explore BV&Bs—INSIGHT: _____

_____

_____

_____

_____

_____

Step 4 confirm passion—INSIGHT: _____

_____

_____

_____

Step 5 proclaim vision—INSIGHT: _____

_____

_____

_____

Step 6 design strategic plan—INSIGHT: _____

_____

_____

_____

Step 7 inventory assets—INSIGHT: _____

_____

_____

_____

_____

Step 8 build network—INSIGHT: _____

_____

_____

_____

_____

_____

Step 9 brand identity—INSIGHT: _____

_____

_____

_____

_____

_____

_____

Step 10 execute plan—INSIGHT: _____

_____

_____

Step 11 evaluate journey—INSIGHT: _____

_____

_____

_____

Step 12 innovate/reinvent—INSIGHT: _____

_____

_____

_____

PERSONAL STRATEGIC VISIONING

Document each section of your personal strategic visioning exercise and transfer it to the worksheet that follows. Keep it with you and reflect upon it periodically to stay on track with your Encore Leadership transformation. (Refer to process book, pages 95–102.)

PERSONAL STRATEGIC

Name:

VISION		
MISSION		
OBJECTIVES	1. 2. 3. 4. 5.	
ST GOALS (2___)	1.	2.
MT GOALS (2___-2___)	1.	2.
LT GOALS (2___+)	1.	
STRATEGIES	1. 2. 3. 4. 5. 6. 7.	
VALUES	1. 2. 3. 4. 5.	
MEASURES	1. 2. 3. 4. 5.	

VISIONING

Dates: 2___ -2___

3.	4.	5.
3.	4.	5.
2.	3.	4.

©2009, Crystal Stairs, Inc.

PERSONAL STRATEGIC VISIONING WORKSHEET

Time Period _____

Vision	
Mission	
Objectives	1.
	2.
	3.
	4.
	5.
Short Term Goals	1.
	2.
	3.
	4.
	5.
Mid-Term Goals	1.
	2.
	3.
	4.
	5.

Long Term Goals	1.
	2.
	3.
	4.
	5.
Strategies	1.
	2.
	3.
	4.
	5.
	6.
	7.
Values	1.
	2.
	3.
	4.
	5.
Measures	1.
	2.
	3.
	4.
	5.

SECTION III: THE ENCORE LEADERSHIP PROCESS©

BLAIR GOALS QUESTIONS

Document responses to the questions that Gary Blair poses regarding setting goals. (Refer to process book, page 98.)

> **RECOMMENDED READING**
>
> Blair, G. R. (2010). *Everything Counts! 52 Remarkable Ways to Inspire Excellence and Drive Results.* Hoboken, NJ: John Wiley & Sons.

1.

2.

3.

4.

5.

6.

7.

GORDON SUCCESS QUESTIONS

Document responses to the questions that Jullien Gordon poses regarding defining success. (Refer to process book, page 99.)

> **RECOMMENDED READING**
>
> Gordon, J. (2009). *The 8 Cylinders of Success: How to align your personal and professional purpose.* Brooklyn, NY: MVMT.

1.
2.
3.
4.
5.
6.
7.
8.

7. INVENTORY YOUR ASSETS

Step 1 document journey—INSIGHT: _____

_____

_____

Step 2 determine purpose—INSIGHT: _____

_____

_____

Step 3 explore BV&Bs—INSIGHT: _____

_____

_____

Step 4 confirm passion—INSIGHT: _____

_____

_____

Step 5 proclaim vision—INSIGHT: _____

_____

_____

_____

Step 6 design strategic plan—INSIGHT: _____

_____

_____

_____

Step 7 inventory assets—INSIGHT: _____

_____

_____

_____

Step 8 build network—INSIGHT: _____

_____

_____

_____

Step 9 brand identity—INSIGHT: _____

_____

_____

Step 10 execute plan—INSIGHT: _____

_____

_____

Step 11 evaluate journey—INSIGHT: _____

_____

_____

Step 12 innovate/reinvent—INSIGHT: _____

_____

_____

_____

LIFE OPTIONS® ASSESSMENT

Document the key insight and actions from the Life Options® Assessment. (Refer to process book, pages 104–106.)

> **RECOMMENDED READING**
>
> Johnson PhD, R. (2006). *What color is your retirement? The LifeOptions® guidebook to discover, plan and live your retirement dream*. St. Louis, MO: Retirement Options.

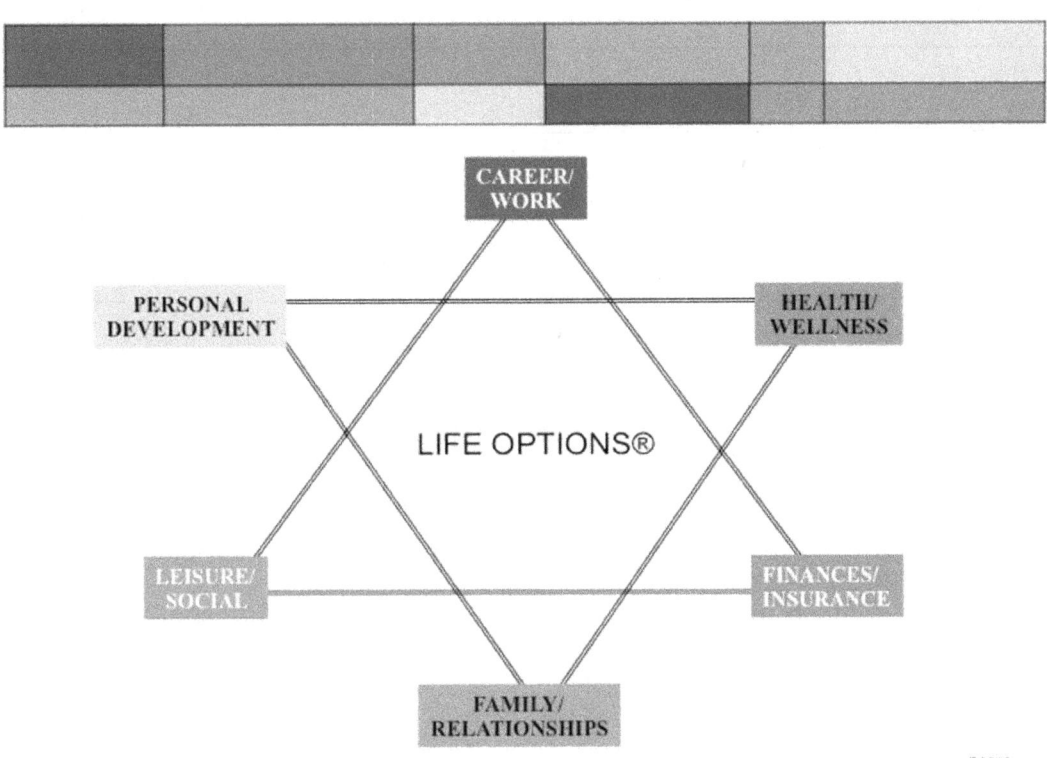

Life Options™ is a registered trademark of Retirement Options

INSIGHT: _____

_____

_____

_____

RECAREER RESULTS

Document the key insight and actions from the ReCareer Assessment. (Refer to process book, page 106.)

Results: _____

TIME ASSESSMENT RESULTS

Document key insight and actions from the Time Assessment. (Refer to process book, page 102.)

Results: _____

_____

_____

_____

_____

_____

_____

_____

_____

_____

_____

_____

_____

_____

JUST SAY NO

Keep a log of the next 10 times you assess a request for your time and you say "No." Discuss the thoughts that led to the "No," your response of gratitude, and the result of your choice to say "No." (Refer to process book, page 104.)

Situation	No with Gratitude Response	Results
1.		
2.		
3.		
4.		
5.		
6.		
7.		
8.		
9.		
10.		

TREASURE

Document key insight and actions from the Life Prospectus Book, *Northern Trust's Legacy Document*, and/or *AARP's Legacy Planning Documents*. (Refer to process book, page 107.)

INSIGHT: _____

_____

_____

_____

_____

_____

_____

_____

_____

_____

_____

_____

_____

8. BUILD YOUR NETWORK

Step 1 document journey—INSIGHT: _____

_____

_____

_____

Step 2 determine purpose—INSIGHT: _____

_____

_____

_____

Step 3 explore BV&Bs—INSIGHT: _____

_____

_____

_____

Step 4 confirm passion—INSIGHT: _____

_____

_____

_____

Step 5 proclaim vision—INSIGHT: _____

_____

_____

_____

Step 6 design strategic plan—INSIGHT: _____

_____

_____

_____

Step 7 inventory assets—INSIGHT: _____

_____

_____

_____

Step 8 build network—INSIGHT: _____

_____

_____

_____

_____

Step 9 brand identity—INSIGHT: _____

_____

_____

_____

Step 10 execute plan—INSIGHT: _____

_____

_____

_____

Step 11 evaluate journey—INSIGHT: _____

_____

_____

_____

Step 12 innovate/reinvent—INSIGHT: _____

_____

_____

_____

ELEVATOR SPEECH

How would you introduce yourself in 30 seconds to someone who asks, "What do you do?" An elevator speech provides a quick, consistent description of who you are and what you do. Use the following format to develop your speech and practice it for flawless flow the next time you're asked.

I am _____ the _____.

I work with _____ who want to _____

and with _____ who want to _____.

Elevator speech notes: _____

_____

_____

_____

_____

_____

_____

_____

_____

WALKER-ROBERTSON NETWORKING TIPS

Write down 3 steps from Cheryl Walker-Robertson's networking tips (Walker-Robertson, 2011, 95 – 106) that you will focus on to strengthen your networking skills. (Refer to process book, pages 108 and 109.)

> **RECOMMENDED READING**
>
> Walker-Robertson, C. (2011). *Networking with Civility: The Ultimate Business Tool. The Power of Civility*. San Francisco, CA: Thrive Publishing.

1.

2.

3.

CIRCLES OF INFLUENCE

Identify key circles of influential people in your life by naming each circle and jotting down the names of the individuals whom you consider key members of that circle of influence. Examples of circles may include: Family, Friends, School Groups, Business Colleagues, Organizations, Community, etc. (Refer to process book, pages 109 and 110.)

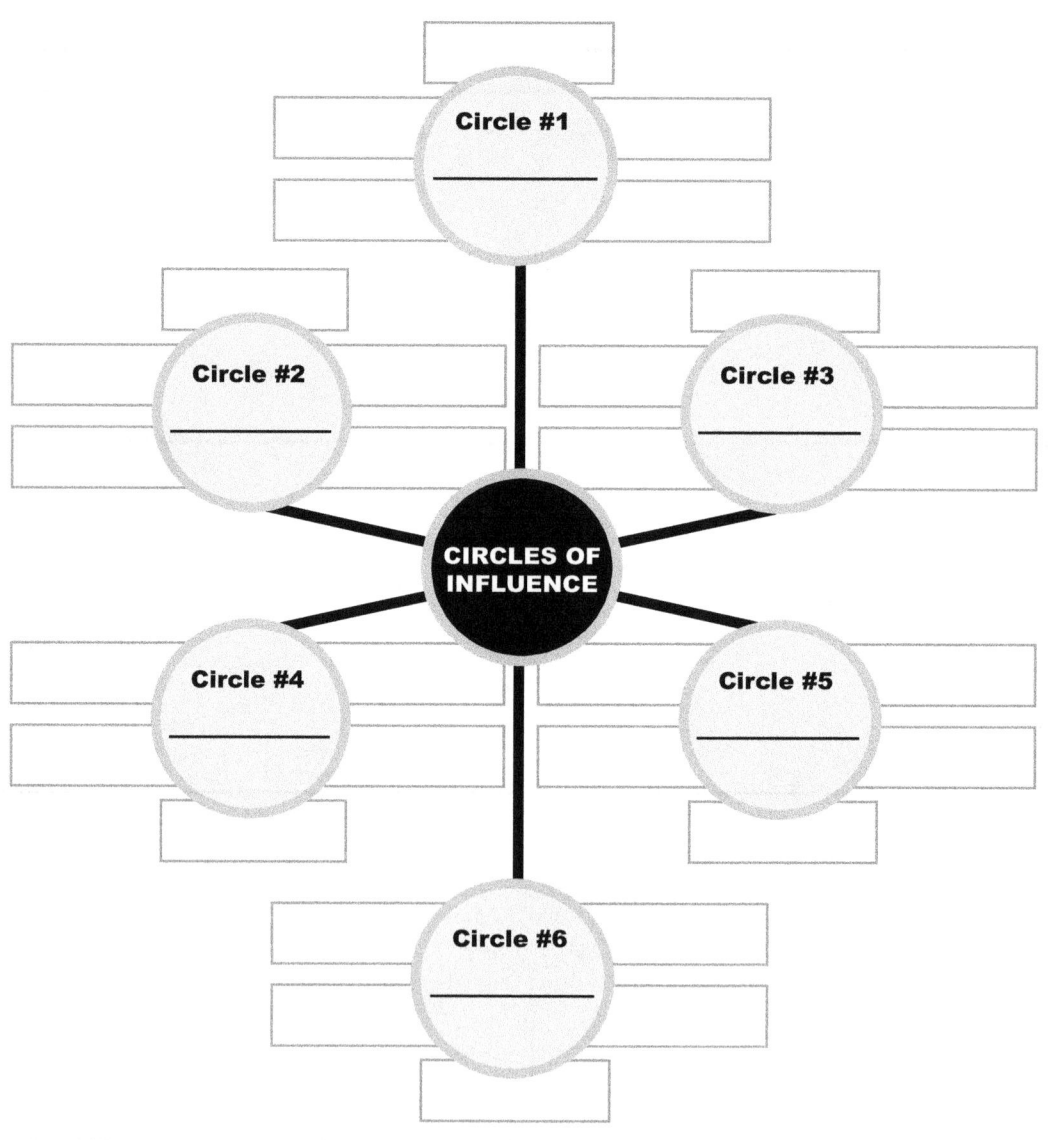

SECTION III: THE ENCORE LEADERSHIP PROCESS©

What actions will you take to strengthen your circles of influence?	
Circle 1:	1.
	2.
	3.
Circle 2:	1.
	2.
	3.
Circle 3:	1.
	2.
	3.
Circle 4:	1.
	2.
	3.
Circle 5:	1.
	2.
	3.
Circle 6:	1.
	2.
	3.

BOARD OF ADVISORS

Who sits at your table as your **_Board of Advisors_**? What is the key area of advice and counsel that you seek in respect to each member of your **_Board_**? Identify your **_Board_** and document the actions you will take to strengthen the relationships with your **_Board_**.

Actions to strengthen relationships with ***Board of Advisors***: _____

ENDORSEMENT

The power of endorsement, as you transform into your Encore Leadership life, can be very important. Document your plan to continue to gain endorsement as shared by Judy Suiter. (Refer to process book, pages 113–115.)

> **RECOMMENDED READING**
>
> Suiter, J. (2003). *The Ripple Effect: How the Global Model of Endorsement Opens Doors to Success.* Peachtree City, GA: Competitive Edge, Inc.

Plan to continue to gain endorsement: _____

_____

_____

_____

_____

_____

_____

_____

_____

_____

9. BRAND YOUR IDENTITY

Step 1 document journey—INSIGHT: _____

_____

_____

Step 2 determine purpose—INSIGHT: _____

_____

_____

Step 3 explore BV&Bs—INSIGHT: _____

_____

_____

Step 4 confirm passion—INSIGHT: _____

_____

_____

_____

SECTION III: THE ENCORE LEADERSHIP PROCESS©

Step 5 proclaim vision—INSIGHT: _____

_____

_____

Step 6 design strategic plan—INSIGHT: _____

_____

_____

Step 7 inventory assets—INSIGHT: _____

_____

_____

Step 8 build network—INSIGHT: _____

_____

_____

_____

Step 9 brand identity—INSIGHT: _____

_____

_____

Step 10 execute plan—INSIGHT: _____

_____

_____

Step 11 evaluate journey—INSIGHT: _____

_____

_____

Step 12 innovate/reinvent—INSIGHT: _____

_____

_____

_____

CLARKE'S PERSONAL BRAND MODEL

Use Ginny Clarke's Personal Brand Model to THINK about your **Brand**. How would you describe each component as it relates to your past and your future endeavors. (Refer to process book, page 119.)

> **RECOMMENDED READING**
>
> Clarke, G., & Garrett, E. (2011). *Career Mapping: Charting Your Course in the New World of Work.* New York, NY: Morgan James Publishing.

COMPONENT	PRESENT DESCRIPTION	FUTURE DESCRIPTION

BRAND COACHING QUESTIONS

Review and respond to the Encore Leadership *Brand Coaching Questions*. (Refer to process book, pages 120 and 121.)

BRANDING QUESTIONS
1.
2.
3.
4.
5.
6.
7.
8.
9.
10.
11.
12.
13.
14.

SAMUEL'S BRANDING CHECKLIST

Review David Samuel's 65 Proven Branding Strategies (section on Branding) and select 3 actions from tips 25–57 on which you will focus for the next 10 days. Document your results in the chart that follows. (Refer to process book, pages 152–154.)

Branding Tip	Action and Results
1.	
2.	
3.	

SOCIAL MEDIA OPTIMIZATION

Assess where you are with social media tools using the suggestions in Phase 3: Reinvest, Step 9. Brand Identity of the *Encore Leadership* process book. (Refer to process book, pages 122–124.)

SUGGESTION	STATUS	ACTION
1.		
2.		
3.		
4.		
5.		
6.		

SUGGESTION (con't)	STATUS	ACTION
7.		
8.		
9.		
10.		
11.		
12.		

10. EXECUTE YOUR PLAN

Step 1 document journey—INSIGHT: _____

_____

_____

Step 2 determine purpose—INSIGHT: _____

_____

_____

Step 3 explore BV&Bs—INSIGHT: _____

_____

_____

Step 4 confirm passion—INSIGHT: _____

_____

_____

_____

Step 5 proclaim vision—INSIGHT: _____

_____

_____

_____

Step 6 design strategic plan—INSIGHT: _____

_____

_____

_____

Step 7 inventory assets—INSIGHT: _____

_____

_____

_____

Step 8 build network—INSIGHT: _____

_____

_____

_____

Step 9 brand identity—INSIGHT: _____

_____

_____

_____

Step 10 execute plan—INSIGHT: _____

_____

_____

_____

Step 11 evaluate journey—INSIGHT: _____

_____

_____

_____

Step 12 innovate/reinvent—INSIGHT: _____

_____

_____

_____

COMFORT ZONE

List at least 10 undertakings that you consider routine or a consistently planned event or activity. To the right of each entry on the chart that follows, please jot down a different way to accomplish the routine or to expand your horizons by shifting to a different approach. For example: ROUTINE — Volunteer at Meals on Wheels. SHIFT from packaging food to delivering the meals and meeting the people whom you are helping. (Refer to process book, page 125.)

ROUTINE	SHIFT
1	
2	
3	
4	
5	
6	
7	
8	
9	
10	

THINK

As a man THINKeth, so he will become. Write down your thoughts as to what you hope to become. Include dates and examples to bring it to the forefront of your THINKing. (Refer to process book, pages 54 and 126.)

THINK _____

_____

_____

_____

_____

_____

_____

_____

_____

_____

_____

_____

_____

_____

25 THINGS TO DO NOW

What resonates to you as critical actions that you can do to transform your time, talent and treasure? Consolidate your thoughts onto the sheet of Actions that follows that you can complete NOW. Start with a list of 25 actions and segment into time categories such as today, tomorrow, next week, next month, next year, etc. You can include actions from previous exercises or just brainstorm and see what lands on this worksheet.

ACTIONS
1.
2.
3.
4.
5.
6.
7.
8.
9.
10.
11.
12.
13.
14.
15.
16.
17.
18.
19.
20.
21.
22.
23.
24.
25.

SECTION III: THE ENCORE LEADERSHIP PROCESS©

11. EVALUATE YOUR JOURNEY

Step 1 document journey—INSIGHT: _____

_____

_____

Step 2 determine purpose—INSIGHT: _____

_____

_____

Step 3 explore BV&Bs—INSIGHT: _____

_____

_____

Step 4 confirm passion—INSIGHT: _____

_____

_____

_____

Step 5 proclaim vision—INSIGHT: _____

_____

_____

Step 6 design strategic plan—INSIGHT: _____

_____

_____

Step 7 inventory assets—INSIGHT: _____

_____

_____

Step 8 build network—INSIGHT: _____

_____

_____

_____

Step 9 brand identity—INSIGHT: _____

_____

_____

_____

Step 10 execute plan—INSIGHT: _____

_____

_____

_____

Step 11 evaluate journey—INSIGHT: _____

_____

_____

_____

Step 12 innovate/reinvent—INSIGHT: _____

_____

_____

_____

SECTION III: THE ENCORE LEADERSHIP PROCESS©

EVALUATE YOUR TRANSFORMATION

Assess your transformation by utilizing the evaluation criteria presented by Leider. (Refer to process book, pages 127 and 128.)

> **RECOMMENDED READING**
>
> Leider, R. J., & Shapiro, D. A. (2012). *Repacking Your Bags: Lighten Your Load For the Good Life.* San Francisco, CA: Berrett-Koehler Publishers, Inc.

EVALUATION CRITERIA	ASSESSMENT
1	
2	
3	
4	
5	
6	
7	
8	

SECTION III: THE ENCORE LEADERSHIP PROCESS©

REPACKED BAG

List items that you have historically taken on your journey in life that you will eliminate as you transform your life. This may be a great time to donate part of your wardrobe, downsize your home, move to a new geography, or tackle a project that has been on your "to-do" list for a long time. (Refer to process book, pages 127 and 128.)

Repacked Bag _____

_____

_____

_____

_____

_____

_____

_____

_____

_____

_____

_____

12. INNOVATE AND REINVENT

Step 1 document journey—INSIGHT: _____

_____

_____

Step 2 determine purpose—INSIGHT: _____

_____

_____

Step 3 explore BV&Bs—INSIGHT: _____

_____

_____

Step 4 confirm passion—INSIGHT: _____

_____

_____

_____

Step 5 proclaim vision—INSIGHT: _____

_____

_____

Step 6 design strategic plan—INSIGHT: _____

_____

_____

Step 7 inventory assets—INSIGHT: _____

_____

_____

Step 8 build network—INSIGHT: _____

_____

_____

Step 9 brand identity—INSIGHT: _____

Step 10 execute plan—INSIGHT: _____

Step 11 evaluate journey—INSIGHT: _____

Step 12 innovate/reinvent—INSIGHT: _____

What has amazed me most about the Encore Leadership journey is the freedom to continually innovate and to explore new frontiers. It often includes new partners and new experiences. It keeps my THINKing fresh and my head, heart and hands excited about "What's Next." Describe what you want to change as you approach the opportunity to **innovate** and **reinvent** your life.

_____

_____

_____

_____

_____

_____

_____

_____

_____

_____

_____

_____

SECTION III: THE ENCORE LEADERSHIP PROCESS©

SECTION IV:

GETTING STARTED

SECTION IV

10 Steps to Get You Started

1. Listen to the Encore Leadership Recording at www.EncoreLeadership.com
2. Make sure to read the following books and take notes in your *Encore Leadership Workbook* and/or *Journal*:
   a. *Encore Leadership: Transforming Time, Talent and Treasure into a Legacy that Matters* (Herein referred to as the process book.)
   b. *Reclaiming Your Place at the Fire*
   c. *Repacking Your Bags*
3. Complete the Encore Leadership Assessment and Dashboard
4. Complete and read the following assessments and associated book:
   a. Life Options and/or Retirement Options
   b. The Good Life Inventory
   c. *Putting Purpose to Work: A Guide to Writing Your Purpose Statement*
5. Engage an Encore Leadership Coach at www.EncoreLeadership.com
6. Attend an Encore Leadership Summit in your Geography or a meeting of an Encore Leadership Summit Sponsoring Organization
7. Join one or more Encore Leadership Communities of Engagement
8. Accept the invitation to join The Global Institute for Innovative and Collaborative THINKing (TGIFiACT) if requested
9. Write a chapter in an upcoming Encore Leadership book or write a book
10. Stay Connected!

Register online at www.EncoreLeadership.com and join other Encore Leaders, people committed to their daily journey of making a difference.

ENCORE LEADERSHIP DASHBOARD

Record your progress on the Dashboard and determine your next steps.

PHASE	STEP	INSIGHT	DOCUMENTS	BLOG	STATUS	NOTES
TTP		Accountability Partner/Cohort EL Mindset TTP Questions	Transition Journey Dash Exercise Life Line Bucket List	O O O O	O	
RE-EXAMINE	1. Document Journey	EL Definition Testament	EL Assessment EL Executive Forum EL Coaching Plan/Goals EL Dashboard	O O O O	O	
	2. Determine Purpose	Strangest Secret Card	Life Purpose Worksheet Purpose Driven Life Work 10 Goals for EL	O O O	O	
	3. Explore Behavior Values Beliefs	DiSC Behavior Values Statement "I Believe in…" Statement	DiSC Report Values Report Personal Compass Trust Barometer Communities Template	O O O O O	O	
	4. Confirm Passion	Attitude Shifts Statement Passion Statement	Exercise Templates Passion Template Risk Analysis Template	O O O	O	
	5. Proclaim Vision	Vision Board Vision Statement	Transition Framework Life Visioning Work Pinterest	O O O	O	
REDEFINE	6. Design PSP Plan	Personal Strategic Plan (PSP)	Website Guide Solid Strategy Template	O O	O	
	7. Inventory Assets	Time, Talent, and Treasure Map	Assessment Report Card Life Prospectus Document Financial Planning Notebook Legal Review Notebook Apple Classes Report	O O O O O	O	
	8. Build Network	Network SCOT Board of Advisors Sphere of Influence	Team 100, Love 25 Relationship Report Reason, Season, Lifetime Endorsement Exercise	O O O O	O	
REINVEST	9. Brand Identity	Brand ID Statement Brand Framework Elevator Speech Article/Chapter Book	Brand Development Event Branding Action Plan Marketing Collateral Social Media Plan	O O O O	O	
	10. EXECUTE	EL Dashboard Assessment Organized Event	Project Plan Barriers Organization Engagement Forum Attendance	O O O O	O	
REIMAGINE	11. Evaluate Plan	THINK Statement EL Journey Blog	EL Checkup Form EL SCOT EL Coaching Plan	O O O	O	
	12. Innovate and Reinvent	TTP Questions	TGIFiACT FELLOWS Invite EL Legacy Sessions Intellectual Stimulation Community Of Engagement	O O O O	O	
		EL WORKBOOK	EL JOURNAL			

DATE: _____

©2012 Crystal Stairs, Inc.

NEXT STEPS

1. _____

_____

_____

_____

_____

_____

2. _____

_____

_____

_____

_____

_____

3. _____

_____

_____

_____

_____

ENCORE LEADERSHIP ASSESSMENTS

Assessment Report Card			
ASSESSMENT	**RESULTS**	**DATE**	**NOTES/ACTIONS**
Encore Leadership			
Behavior			
Personality			
Values			
The Good Life Inventory			
Time Management			
Listening			
Work Expectations			
Retirement Options			
Life Options®			
Coping and Stress			
Leadership			
Other			
Other			

THE COACH APPROACH

Crystal Stairs, Inc. has adopted a method of coaching Encore Leaders called *Visible Coaching*. A team of certified coaches is at the ready to offer this unique coaching opportunity to individuals who seek to have accountability through action. The coaching engagement clarifies specific goals and then focuses on achieving them. Select your coach today from our available team at www.EncoreLeadership.com.

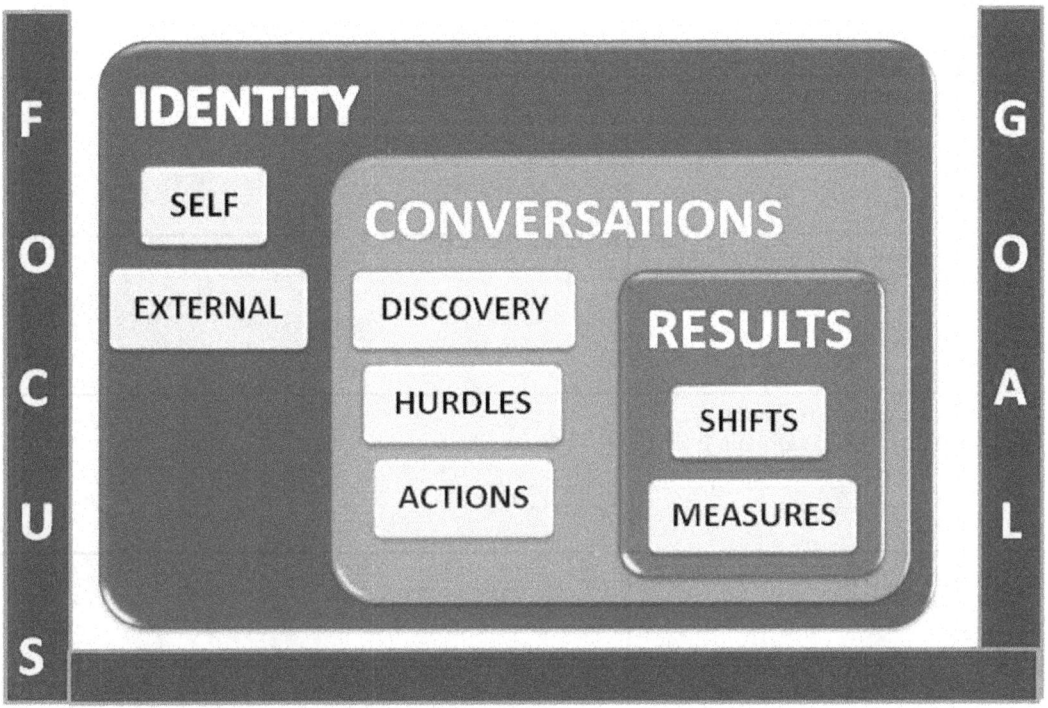

Coaching tools included in this workbook are:

- Coaching "It"
- Coaching Personal Profile (Completion is optional)
- 10 Goals to Reach in the Next 90 Days
- Coaching Session Preparation Form
- Coaching Conversation Format

COACHING "IT"

Identifying the focus for coaching can be a very challenging task. The "elephant in the room" that raises the coaching flag must be acknowledged with openness and honesty that often comes from various sources. Once "it" is identified, taking the steps necessary to coach "it" becomes an opportunity for transformation. Being ready to tackle "it" is as important as identifying "it". THINK about the following questions to determine if you are ready to engage in a coaching relationship.

1.	What do you think "it" is?	
2.	Who has shared "it" with you?	
3.	Do you think it is important to work on "it"?	
4.	Will you dedicate regularly scheduled time to work on "it"?	
5.	What are the potential benefits of working on "it"?	
6.	Are you open to uncovering the mask that is sheltering "it"?	
7.	What is your next step to start working on "it"?	

COACHING PERSONAL PROFILE

First Name		Last Name	
Address		City	
State/Province		Postal Code	
Country		Company	
Title		Home Phone	
Work Phone		Work Extension	
Mobile Phone		Fax Phone	
Email		2nd Email	
Occupation		Referred By	
Birthday		Marital Status	
Religious affiliation		Spouse Name	
Anniversary		Children's Names and Birthdays	

Your Goals:

What are the 3 biggest changes you want to make in your life in the next 3 months?

1. _____
2. _____
3. _____

What are the 3 biggest changes you want to make in your life over the next 3 years?

1. _____
2. _____
3. _____

What do you most want to achieve? And do you feel ready for it?

Your History:

What do you consider to be your 3 greatest accomplishments to date?

1. _____
2. _____
3. _____

SECTION IV: GETTING STARTED

What is the toughest obstacle in your life that you have had to overcome? _____
_____

Who are or have been your major role models? _____

Have you worked with a coach before or been in a similar one-on-one adult relationship (e.g. tennis coach, piano teacher, therapist)? If yes, what worked well for you and what did not work in the relationship(s)? _____
_____

What major transitions have you had in the past 2 years? Entering or approaching a new decade, a new relationship, a new job, a new role, a new residence, change in children's ages/stages, etc.? _____
_____

Improvements:

List improvements you want to make in the following areas of your life.
Family/home life: _____
Financial situation: _____
Career or business life: _____
Personal character: _____
Relationships: _____
Leisure time: _____
Self-care: _____
Learning: _____

Your Life:

Who are the key people in your life, and what do they provide you? _____
_____

Is your life of your choosing? If not, which parts are being chosen for you? _____
_____

What is your favorite part of your typical day? _____

What is your least favorite part of your typical day? _____

Looking at the past 6 months of your life, do you like the direction in which your life is moving? _____
_____

On a scale of 1 to 10 — 10 being highest — rate the amount of stress in your life right now. _____

What are your primary stressors? _____

_____

List five issues that you are tolerating or putting up with in your life at present. (For examples: info. you can't find, clutter, rude friends, poor lighting, tight shoes, dented car, job dissatisfaction, dead plants, broken equipments, old appliances, etc.)

1. _____
2. _____
3. _____
4. _____
5. _____

Yourself:

List 5 adjectives that describe you at your best.

1. _____
2. _____
3. _____
4. _____
5. _____

List 5 adjectives that describe you at your worst.

1. _____
2. _____
3. _____
4. _____
5. _____

What are your 3 major concerns/fears about yourself?

1. _____
2. _____
3. _____

SECTION IV: GETTING STARTED

What are your 3 major concerns/fears about life?

1. _____
2. _____
3. _____

What motivates you? _____

What are you learning/accepting about yourself at present? _____

Coaching You:

What would you like your coach to do if you get behind on your goals? _____

Do you understand that if you miss a coaching session without notice, your coach will be unable to make it up? _____

How will you know that you are receiving value (i.e. your money's worth) from the coaching process? ___
_____

Are you able and willing to pay a monthly coaching fee? _____

What types of coaching and/or personality approaches discourage you or take away motivation from you? _____

Which alterations, if any, in your coach's natural communication style do you wish he or she would make when working with you? _____

Do you enjoy self-assessments and improvement programs? _____
_____

Here are ways coaching clients use a coach. Which appeal to you?
- ☐ Brainstorming strategies together
- ☐ Support, encouragement and validation
- ☐ Insight into who you are and your potential
- ☐ Painting a vision of what you can become or accomplish
- ☐ Exploring and removing blocks and obstacles to your success
- ☐ Accountability; checking up on goals
- ☐ Working through self-improvement programs together
- ☐ Suggesting or designing action steps

Potential and Possibility:

Do you have a personal or professional vision? If so, what is it? _____

_____

What would you like to contribute to the world? _____

What do you think is NOT possible to achieve in your lifetime that you wish you could? _____

_____

What is a dream or goal you have given up on? _____

What part of yourself, if any, have you given up on? _____

On a scale of 1 to 10 — 10 being highest — rate the quality of your life today. _____

If you reach the age of 95 by continuing to live your life and order your time exactly the way you do right now, what regrets do you think you will have? (Tip: complete the statement "I wish I had…") Do not include things from the past—only things you will regret if you continue your exact present path. _____

_____

_____

Your Tastes:

Favorite color(s): _____

Style of decorating or clothing (For example: Traditional, Sporty, Classic, Romantic, Dramatic, Contemporary, Eclectic — anything that describes your style): _____

_____

Collections (if you have any): _____

Hobbies: _____

Favorite authors, types of books or magazines: _____

_____

Types of music and favorite artists you ENJOY: _____

_____

Foods, drinks, and flavors: _____

Scents (For example: vanilla, berry, Old Spice, floral, woodsy, "new car," etc.): _____

_____

SECTION IV: GETTING STARTED

10 GOALS TO REACH IN THE NEXT 90 DAYS

What are the goals you most want to set for yourself for the next 90 days? Please select only those goals that you really want to achieve, not the ones you should, could, ought, or might want to achieve. Look deep inside yourself, and then write down your 10 personal and professional goals and discuss these with your coach. When you set the right goals for yourself, you should feel excited, a little nervous, ready and willing to go for it! Don't select the goals you historically have chosen, but never reached, unless you're in a much better position to reach them now.

Start Date	Finish Date	The Specific Measurable Goal	Completed
_____	_____	1._____	_____
_____	_____	2._____	_____
_____	_____	3._____	_____
_____	_____	4._____	_____
_____	_____	5._____	_____
_____	_____	6._____	_____
_____	_____	7._____	_____
_____	_____	8._____	_____
_____	_____	9._____	_____
_____	_____	10._____	_____

Please develop a 3-step action plan or strategy for each goal and fine-tune this with your Encore Leadership coach.

What are the personal/professional benefits to you of accomplishing each of these goals?

1._____

2._____

3._____

4._____

5._____

COACHING SESSION PREPARATION FORM

Name	
Date of Call	
FOCUS (Agenda)	
REALITY GOAL *Accomplished or Learned* *Didn't Accomplish*	
DISCOVERY QUESTIONING 1. 2. 3. *Challenges/Concerns*	
ACTION(s)	
REMOVE BARRIERS *Obstacles* *Tolerations*	
RECAP Grateful For	

COACHING CONVERSATION

FOCUS	
CURRENT REALITY	
GOAL	
INITIATE DISCOVERY	LISTEN TO THE POINT OF DISAPPEARING INTO COACHABLE MOMENTS. PROVIDE FEEDBACK, REQUESTS, AND QUESTIONS. **THREE POWERFUL QUESTIONS THAT WILL CAUSE A SHIFT:** 1. 2. 3.
ACT	
REMOVE BARRIERS	
ACKNOWLEDGE — CELEBRATE	
RECAP	

ENCORE LEADERSHIP COMMUNITIES OF ENGAGEMENT

Sign up to join other Encore Leaders, successful people committed to making a difference in their daily journey and leaving a legacy that matters. To join, register at www.EncoreLeadership.com. As you progress with engagement as an Encore Leader, expect to receive an invitation to join The Global Institute for Innovative and Collaborative THINKing (TGIFiACT). The designation of Encore Leader Coach and Encore Leader Fellow will be extended to those of you who truly set an example for others to follow and who meet the criteria for these designations.

Communities of engagement are forums and discussion groups where you can share interests, stories, and engagement opportunities. These communities are managed as social media groups with periodic events to convene conversations. The current communities are:

- Educator – Teaching others
- Education - Learning
- Education Advocacy – Impacting the education system
- Spiritual
- Philanthropy
- Foundation Leadership
- Foundation Creation
- Foundation Support
- Entrepreneur
- Coaching
- Author
- Publisher
- Family Historian
- Health
- Mentoring
- Golf
- Travel
- Other Personal Interests

STAY CONNECTED...

To find out all the news and updates associated with Encore Leaders and Encore Leadership, sign up for our updates on various platforms. Our website, www.EncoreLeadership.com will be the central place for our static news, but we will aggressively embrace the immediacy of Twitter, Facebook, and other social media tools. We will evolve communication channels that will connect and engage like-minded transitioning individuals and organizations.

Blog and share your stories with Encore Leaders. Participate in an authored book with your expertise in a chapter. Support the books that will emerge from The Global Institute for Innovative and Collaborative THINKing (TGIFiACT). Share our stories with friends and associates, who will be energized to pursue or to step up their Encore Leadership life.

There are several specific objectives that the Institute will provide to support Encore Leaders. These include:

- Encourage the creation of environments for courageous conversations;
- Connect communities of engagement networks to leverage resources;
- Establish regional hubs and a national network of Encore Leaders;
- Publish stories to share wisdom;
- Build platforms to inspire entrepreneurship, angel investments, philanthropy and service endeavors;
- Partner with organizations exemplifying innovative engagement to solve issues impacting society;
- Extend the life cycle of membership in organizations through agendas that matter and attract Encore Leaders so they are available to reach back and give back to the organization;
- Establish profitable pursuits for Encore Leaders – financial, emotional, physical, spiritual and mattering.

RECOMMENDED READING AND RESOURCES

Tearte, J. (2013). *Encore Leadership: Transforming Time, Talent and Treasure into a Legacy that Matters.* Atlanta, GA: Crystal Stairs Publishers.

Tearte, J. (2013). *Encore Leadership Journal.* Atlanta, GA: Crystal Stairs Publishers.

Foster, J. M. (2009). Cracking the Transition Code: A Paradigmatic Framework of Competencies that Construct the Reality of 50+ Black Executive Transitions. *Dissertation, 267* (UMI No. 3367130).

Arthur, M. (2007). *A Black Man Thinking: Raising Children* (Vol. 1). Oak Park, IL: A Black Man Thinking, LLC.

Beckwith, M. B. (2008). *Life Visioning: A Step-by-Step Process for Realizing Your Highest Potential.* Boulder, CO: Sounds True.

Bell Ph.D, E. L. (2010). *Career GPS: Strategies for Women Navigating the New Corporate Landscape.* New York, NY: HarperCollins Publishers.

Blair, G. R. (2010). *Everything Counts! 52 Remarkable Ways to Inspire Excellence and Drive Results.* Hoboken, NJ: John Wiley & Sons.

Bourke, D. H. (2006). *Second Calling: Finding Passion & Purpose for the rest of your life.* Brentwood, TN: Integrity Publishers.

Bridges, W. (1999). *Managing Transitions: Making the Most of Change.* New York, NY: HarperCollins Publishers.

Bridges, W. (2004). *Transitions: Making Sense of Life's Changes — Strategies for coping with the difficult, painful, and confusing times in your life* (Revised 25th Anniversary Edition). Cambridge, MA: Da Capo Press, A Member of the Perseus Book Group.

Buford, B. (1994). *Half Time: Changing Your Game Plan from Success to Significance.* Grand Rapids, MI: Zondervan.

Buford, B. (2000). *Halftime: Changing Your Life Plan from Success to Significance.* Grand Rapids, MI: Zondervan.

Clarke, G., & Garrett, E. (2011). *Career Mapping: Charting Your Course in the New World of Work.* New York, NY: Morgan James Publishing.

SECTION IV: GETTING STARTED

Clinton, B. (2007). *Giving: How Each of Us Can Change the World.* New York, NY: Alfred A. Knopf.

Cobbs, P. (2005). *My American Life: From rage to entitlement.* New York, NY: Altria Books.

Coleman, H. (2006). *Empowering Yourself: The rules of the game* (Original Work Published 1996 ed.). Atlanta, GA: Coleman Publishing.

Covey, S. M. (2006). *The Speed of Trust: The One Thing That Changes Everything.* New York, NY: Simon & Schuster, Inc.

Daniels, C. (2005). Pioneers. *Fortune,* 152 (4), 72-88.

De Bono, E. (2008). *Creativity Workout: 62 Exercises to Unlock Your Most Creative Ideas.* Berkeley, CA: Ulysses Press.

De Bono, E. (2009). *Think! Before It's Too Late.* London, England: Vermilion.

Edelman, M. W. (1992). *The Measure of Our Success: A Letter to My Children and Yours.* Boston, MA: Beacon Press.

Foster, J. M. (2002). *Due North! Strengthen Your Leadership Assets.* Hinsdale, IL: Crystal Stairs Publishers.

Frankl, V. (1963). *Man's Search for Meaning.* New York, NY: Pocket Books.

Gladwell, M. (2000). *The Tipping Point: How little things can make a big difference.* Boston, MA: Little, Brown and Company.

Goodly, T. W. (2007). Unfolding the Road Map to Success: A Grounded Theory Study of the Role of Agency and Structure in the Upward Mobility of African American Men. *Dissertation, 304 (UMI No. 3269580).*

Goodman, M. (2008). *Reinventing Retirement: 389 Bright Ideas about Family, Friends, Health, What to Do, and Where to Live.* San Francisco, CA: Chronicle Books, LLC.

Gordon, J. (2009). *Good Excuse Goals: How to End Procrastination and Perfectionism Forever.* Brooklyn, NY: MVMT.

Gordon, J. (2009). *The 8 Cylinders of Success: How to align your personal and professional purpose.* Brooklyn, NY: MVMT.

Harrell, K. (2000). *Attitude is Everything: 10 Life-Changing Steps to Turning Attitude into Action.* New York, NY: Cliff Street Books, an Imprint of HarperCollins Publishers.

Height, D. I. (2010). *Living with Purpose: An Activist's Guide to Listening, Learning and Leading.* Washington, DC: The Dorothy I. Height Education Foundation.

Hitzges, V., *International Motivational Strategist and Best Selling Author.* (2013, September 26) Telephone Interview.

Hobson, A., & Clarke, J. (1997). *The Power of Passion: Achieve Your Own Everests.* Calgary, AB, Canada: Stewart Publishing.

Hunter, N., & Chambers-Chima, D. (2005). *Choose to Lead: Advice, Tools, and Strategies for Women from Women.* Hilton Head, SC: Cameo Publications, LLC.

Johnson, M. D. (2008). *Brand Me®. Make Your Mark: Turn Passion into Profit.* Reynoldsburg, OH: Ambassador Press, LLC.

Johnson, PhD, R. (2006). *What color is your retirement? The LifeOptions® guidebook to discover, plan and live your retirement dream.* St. Louis, MO: Retirement Options.

Johnson Ph.D, R. (2009). *ReCareer, find your authentic work: How to discover and pursue a purposeful ReCareer that stimulates your mind, fires your heart, and feeds your spirit.* St. Louis, MO: Richard P. Johnson.

Kimbro, D. (1998). *What Makes the Great Great: Strategies for Extraordinary Achievement.* New York, NY: Doubleday.

Kloser, C. (2012). *A Daily Dose of Love: Everyday Inspiration to Help You Remember What Your Heart Already Knows.* York, PA: Transformation Books.

Kloser, C. (2013). *Pebbles in the Pond: Transforming the World One Person at a Time* (Wave Two). York, PA: Transformation Books.

Leider, R. J., & Shapiro, D. A. (2012). *Repacking Your Bags: Lighten Your Load For the Good Life.* San Francisco, CA: Berrett-Koehler Publishers, Inc.

Leider, R. J. (2010). *The Power of Purpose: Find Meaning, Live Longer, Better.* San Francisco, CA: Berrett-Koehler Publishers, Inc.

Leider, R. J., & Shapiro, D. A. (2004). *Claiming your place at the fire: Living the second half of your life on purpose.* San Francisco, CA: Berrett-Koehler Publishers, Inc.

Leider, R. J., & Shapiro, D. A. (2001). *Whistle While You Work: Heeding Your Life's Calling.* San Francisco, CA: Berrett-Koehler Publishers, Inc.

Lindbergh, A. M. (1955, 1975, 1983, 2003). *Gift from the Sea.* New York, NY: Random House.

Loehr, J. (2007). *The Power of Story: Change your story, change your destiny in business and in life.* New York, NY: Simon & Schuster, Inc.

Losier, M. J. (2003, 2006). *Law of Attraction: The Science of Attracting More of What You Want and Less of What You Don't.* New York, NY: Wellness Central, Hatchette Book Group.

Martin, J. H. (2002, 2009). *Fulfilled: The Art and Joy of Balanced Living.* Chicago, IL: Nu Vision Media.

Maxwell, J. C. (2001). *The Right to Lead: A Study in Character and Courage.* Nashville, TN: J. Countryman®, a division of Thomas Nelson, Inc.

Maxwell, J. (2004). *Make Today Count: The Secret of Your Success is Determined by Your Daily Agenda.* New York, NY: Center Street, Hachette Book Group.

Maxwell, J. (2003). *Thinking for a Change: 11 Ways Highly Successful People Approach Life and Work.* New York, NY: Warner Books.

Mueller, R. K. (1978). *Career conflict: Management's inelegant dysfunction.* Lexington, MA: D. C. Heath and Company.

Neff, T., & Citrin, J. (1999). *Lessons from the Top: The Search for America's Best Business Leaders.* New York, NY: Doubleday.

Nightingale, E. (1956). *The Strangest Secret. Original Recording.* Wheeling, IL: Nightingale-Conant.

Northern Trust. (2008, 2011). *Legacy: Conversations About Wealth Transfer.* Deerfield Beach, FL: TriMark Press.

Pausch, R. with Jeffrey Zaslow. (2008). *The Last Lecture.* New York, NY: Hyperion.

Peters, T. (2003). *Re-imagine! Business Excellence in a Disruptive Age.* (M. Slind, Ed.). London, England: Dorling Kindersley Limited.

Peters, T. (1999). *the brand you 50: Fifty ways to transform yourself from an "employee" into a brand that shouts distinction, commitment, and passion.* New York, NY: Alfred A. Knopf.

Petrilli, L. (2012, January 12). *An Introvert's Guide to Networking.* Retrieved January 14, 2012, from Harvard Business Review: http:///www.lisapetrilli.com/the-introverts-guide/

Qubein, N. R. (1997). *Stairway to Success: The Complete Blueprint for Personal and Professional Achievement.* New York, NY: John Wiley & Sons.

Rath, T. & Clifton Ph.D, D. (2004). *How Full Is Your Bucket? Positive Strategies for Work and Life.* New York, NY: Gallup Press.

Samuel, D. (2006). *Personal Branding Power: 65 Proven Strategies for Accelerated Career Growth.* Atlanta, GA: Lean Forward and Go!

Schultz, P. (2003). *1000 Places To See Before You Die: A Traveler's Life List.* New York, NY: Workman Publishing Company, Inc.

Shickler, S. & Waller, J. (2011). *The 7 Mindsets To Live Your Ultimate Life.* Roswell, GA: Ultimate Life Media, a division of Excent Corporation.

St. John, B. & Deane, D. (2012). *How Great Women Lead: A Mother-Daughter Adventure Into the Lives of Women Shaping the World.* New York, NY: Hachette Book Group.

Suiter, J. (2003). Energizing People: *Unleashing the Power of DiSC.* Peachtree City, GA: Competitive Edge, Inc.

Suiter, J. (2003). *Exploring Values! Releasing the power of attitudes.* Peachtree City, GA: Competitive Edge, Inc.

Suiter, J. (2003). *The Ripple Effect: How the Global Model of Endorsement Opens Doors to Success.* Peachtree City, GA: Competitive Edge, Inc.

Tichy, N. M. (1986). *The Transformational Leader.* New York, NY: John Wiley & Sons.

Tracy, B. (2009). *Reinvention: How to Make the Rest of Your Life the Best of Your Life.* New York, NY: AMACOM.

Walker-Robertson, C. (2011). *Networking with Civility: The Ultimate Business Tool. The Power of Civility* (pp. 95-106). San Francisco, CA: Thrive Publishing.

Warren, R. (2002). *The Purpose Driven Life: What On Earth Am I Here For?* Grand Rapids, MI: Zondervan.

Williams, T. (1994). *The Personal Touch: What You Really Need to Succeed in Today's Fast Paced Business World.* New York, NY: Warner Books, Inc.

SECTION IV: GETTING STARTED

ACKNOWLEDGMENTS

A very special Thank You to my partners in the creation and delivery of this workbook and future programs to support Encore Leaders.

the Ink Studio – Daniel Barrozo
        Graphic Design
        Cover and Book Interior Design
        eBook Conversions
        Editing/Proofreading

Eight:31 Marketing – Anjylla Foster
        Social Media Management
        Website Development
        Teleseminar Management

ABOUT THE AUTHOR

Jylla Moore Tearte, Ph.D. — President and CEO, Corporate Coach U Graduate, Coachville Graduate School of Coaching, Certified Coaching Clinic™ Facilitator, Certified Retirement Coach, Inscape Publishing, Inc. Licensed Distributor, Author of Due North! Strengthen Your Leadership Assets.

Jylla Moore Tearte, PhD was one of IBM's top women executives with more than 20 years of various leadership assignments that spanned the globe. A nationally acclaimed Encore Leader, she is the President and CEO of Crystal Stairs, Inc. and is recognized for her innovative and insightful work with individuals who have been successful and seek to contribute legacy work to society. As COO for Tearte Associates, Jylla manages the Tearte Family Foundation, a portfolio of education partnerships that provide scholarships and grants to designated organizations for their scholars. She has authored several books and processes that enable clients to optimize their time, talent and treasure through collaborative networks of community engagement opportunities and resources. She lives in Atlanta, Georgia with her husband, Curtis.

ABOUT CRYSTAL STAIRS, INC.

Crystal Stairs, Inc. exists to build a network of transformative leaders by coaching pivotal transitions of the leadership maturation life cycle with a core competency of Encore Leaders. The firm offers innovative services focused on talent development and creating legacies that matter. Services include: Encore Leadership and Executive Coaching; assessments; training; consulting and strategic visioning for individuals, corporations, educational institutions, government entities and organizations. Founded in 2000, clients attest to becoming more results-driven, goal oriented, and shifting from success to significant.

For further information, please visit:
www.Crystal-Stairs.com

You can also contact us at:
Crystal Stairs, Inc., P. O Box 12215, Atlanta, GA 30355 USA

Email: Info@Crystal-Stairs.com

We invite you to share your experiences with Encore Leadership. If you find unique information or techniques to extend best practices within this book, please share it. If you have suggestions for additional information to include in this document, please let us know. Together our work will guarantee that this will be an incredible journey. THANKS in advance for your contributions.

Dr. Jylla Moore Tearte, CEO
Crystal Stairs, Inc.

Please visit us to join our network discussions or to request information on the following services:

- Workshops and Seminars (Face-to-face and Webinars)
- Become a best selling book author by contributing to an Encore Leader Chapter Book
- Encore Leadership Coaching
- Assessments

Join the Encore Leadership Movement

- www.EncoreLeadership.com
- www.Twitter.com/DrJylla
- #EncoreLeader
- www.Facebook.com/EncoreLeadership
- www.Pinterest.com/EncoreLeaders/
- www.YouTube.com/DrJylla
- Crystal Stairs, Inc., P.O. Box 12215, Atlanta, GA 30355
- DrJylla@EncoreLeadership.com

Notes:

Notes:

Notes:

Notes:

Notes:

Notes:

Notes:

Notes:

Notes:

Notes:

Notes:

Notes:

Notes:

Notes:

Notes:

Notes:

Notes:

Notes:

Notes:

www.ingramcontent.com/pod-product-compliance
Lightning Source LLC
Chambersburg PA
CBHW081835170426
43199CB00017B/2734